ב"ה

CHALLAH ADVENTURES
FOR THE WHOLE FAMILY

THE
KIDS

BOOK OF
CHALLAH

ROCHIE PINSON

Illustrations by Illustrations by Huxmay (Martina Rosnokova)
Photography by Monica Pinto
Step-by-step kids' photos by Schneur Menaker
Braiding photos, including section cover, by Chavi Werzberger
Design direction and consultation by Esty Raskin
Book design by Rochie Pinson
Recipes edited by Elisheva Taitz
Front of book edited by Elky Raitport

Distributed by
Feldheim Publishers
POB 43163 / Jerusalem, Israel
208 Airport Executive Park / Nanuet, NY 10954
www.feldheim.com

Distributed in Europe by
Lehmanns
+44-0-191-430-0333
info@lehmanns.co.uk
www.lehmanns.co.uk

Distributed in Australia by
Golds World of Judaica
+613 952278775
info@golds.com.au
www.golds.com.au

Printed in China

For my children, the loves of my life.

**Estee and Mendel Konikov,
Mendel, Shua,
and Avraham** שיחיו

And for my crew of little nieces and nephews, שיחיו
those in the book, and those that are not,
you bring so much love and joy into my life!

❧

In honor of the Lubavitcher Rebbe זי״ע
who inspired this book.
He dreamed and campaigned
for the light of Shabbat in every home,
and for every Jewish child
to feel its warmth.

TABLE OF CONTENTS

FOR THE FULL
LIST OF RECIPES,
SEE PAGE 50

SECTION 3: THE RECIPES

SECTION 4: THE SHAPES AND COLORS OF CHALLAH

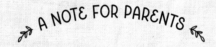

A NOTE FOR PARENTS

"וְהָיָה בַּאֲכָלְכֶם מִלֶּחֶם הָאָרֶץ תָּרִימוּ תְרוּמָה לַה':"
"רֵאשִׁית עֲרִסֹתֵכֶם חַלָּה תָּרִימוּ תְרוּמָה ..."

The Torah tells us, when you eat the bread of the land ... *"reishit arisoteichem
[the beginnings of your dough], lift up as challah"* (Bamidbar 15:19–20).

While it's still a lump of jiggly gluten, not even dreaming of the beautiful braided
masterpiece it will become, take off a little piece of that dough—the gift of challah—and
declare it to be holy.

This gift, called "challah," was given to the priests in the times of our Temple in Jerusalem.
Today, when we separate it and declare it to be challah, it becomes sacred and not for us to
eat. It confers holiness on all of our dough, the braided challah breads it will become,
and all that sustains us. This gift of challah becomes a channel for blessings in our lives.

We don't wait until a house is painted and wallpapered to lay down a foundation. We lay the
foundation when the beauty of what it will be is still a faraway dream. And when we lay the
structural underpinnings well and early, all the beauty that comes later will endure.

The Lubavitcher Rebbe spoke to us about laying a foundation in our lives, based on the
mitzvah of challah. He spoke about the fact that the word *reishit* means the beginning, the
"head" (like Rosh Hashanah). Everything that happens begins in the head.
When we begin with the awareness that "man does not live by bread alone,"
that all of our life and blessings come from the ultimate Source of life and oneness, Hashem
alone, then all that comes from this awareness will be connected to the Source of life,
and be vibrant, true, and set to endure.

Our children are the beauty that is still becoming,
the hearts and homes of the future.
By infusing our nourishment of them with love for the pure soul that they are,
and awareness of their inherent connection to the Divine, we are securing for them a
meaning, connection, and inner joy, and the continuity of thousands of years of Torah, the
tree of life.

*I hope that this book illuminates the hearts of our children,
from the very youngest, to our tweens and teens,
inspiring them on their own delicious adventures into the world of challah,
and into the inner landscape of their soul.*

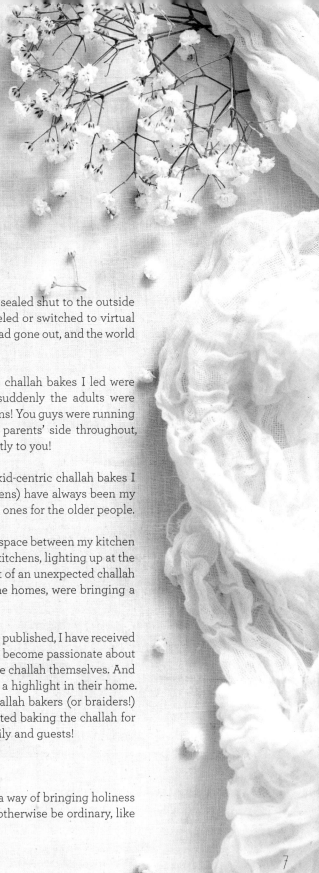

INTRODUCTION

"Sof maaseh b'machshavah techilah."
Everything in creation begins as a thought, an idea, a dream.

So too, this book you hold in your hand.
I remember well the first time the thought of this book came to me.

It was deep in the quarantine of 2020. The doors of our homes were sealed shut to the outside world. All the challah bakes I was scheduled to lead had been canceled or switched to virtual events one by one. The streets were empty, the lights in the big city had gone out, and the world felt scary and dark.

But then, something unexpectedly wonderful happened. While the challah bakes I led were usually for adults and took place in a space outside the home, suddenly the adults were "Zoom"ing from their kitchens and kids were showing up on the screens! You guys were running around, gathering the ingredients, measuring and mixing at your parents' side throughout, totally present and engaged, and I found myself wanting to talk mostly to you!

I've taught challah baking to kids before, lots of times. In fact, the kid-centric challah bakes I lead (like the ones in schools, and for Bat Mitzvahs and sweet sixteens) have always been my favorites! But they always felt like an extra; the main events were the ones for the older people.

And then, one evening, on a virtual challah bake somewhere in cyberspace between my kitchen in New York and your homes in California, seeing all of you in your kitchens, lighting up at the opportunity to make a challah, and laughing excitedly at the thought of an unexpected challah recipe or shape, I realized that you, the kids, tweens, and teens of the homes, were bringing a "fresh-as-Friday-challah" perspective to this delicious mitzvah.

Ever since my first challah cookbook, *Rising! The Book of Challah*, was published, I have received countless messages from parents telling me that their children have become passionate about challah, are pushing them to make challah, and in fact are making the challah themselves. And how, with the enthusiasm they have for this mitzvah, it has become a highlight in their home. Some moms have told me that their kids have become the main challah bakers (or braiders!) of their homes. One niece of mine, from the young age of nine, started baking the challah for Shabbat—now she doesn't miss a week of baking challah for her family and guests!

I could go on and on, but you know what I'm talking about.

Challah isn't like any other regular food we make in the kitchen. It's a way of bringing holiness and meaning into our home, and transforming something that can otherwise be ordinary, like bread, into something extraordinary, like challah!

So now I wrote a book for YOU.

You are the future leaders of our world, you are the ones who will build beautiful homes and families that are solidly grounded in spirit and holiness. Your enthusiasm and love for Shabbat and the baking (and eating!) of challah will be the supercharge that the next generation of our People need to endure and thrive and pass the message onward.

This cookbook is full of fun and original challah recipes, as well as so many ideas of what to do with a challah dough and a baked challah—you can pick a new recipe each week and still be busy with this for years to come. But this book is meant to be more than a collection of fun and cool recipes. I created this book for you, to help you lead the way in making your home one that sparkles with the light of Shabbat. Challah is just the beginning. There is the lighting of the candles, the special table settings, and all the other ways in which we transform our usual living space into a magical Shabbat island.

I wished, I wondered, and I willed this book into being. In a time that felt too dark, I witnessed the joy and light on your hopeful faces, and wished I could spark more of that wonder. I imagined a beautiful book, full of fanciful challah creations, that would be a magic-carpet ride into challah-land. And then, because inspiration is only one percent of any successful project, I spent the next two years bringing this idea to life. Now I can't wait to see the wonderful challah concoctions you cook up, using the ideas in this book as your inspiration to take it even further.

It is my hope and prayer that this book lights you up from the inside, inspiring you to try new things and sparking your most wild challah imaginings.

Most of all, I hope you discover the beauty and peace that Shabbat brings into our homes and our lives, and I certainly hope you get to celebrate it with the most wondrous challahs.
Are you ready to bake? Let the challah adventures begin!

From my kitchen to your hearts with love,

Rochie

New York, August 2022 / Menachem-Av 5782

IN HONOR OF:
Marilyn and Howard Brill
and family שיחיו
שמשון בן לאה · מרים בת חוה
אביבה בת מרים · שלום חיים בן מרים
חיים בן אביבה · שלום בן אביבה
· אורלי בת שרה ·

FOR THE TWEENS & TEENS
& ADULTS AT HEART

This book is called *The KIDS Book of Challah*, but I wrote this with kids of all ages in mind. If you're a tween, a teen, or a young adult, this book is very much for you. In fact, I have a feeling adults are going to love this too.

Some of the recipes may look complicated, but real kids (ages 6–16) tried all the recipes and I know they can be done. The recipes are marked with stars according to difficulty, from one star (easiest) to three stars (most complex), but that might not mean anything to you. You decide which recipes you feel like tackling, and then go for it! Sometimes a recipe is only complex because it has many steps or uses methods like chopping and frying. If you're already proficient in the kitchen and feel comfortable with these techniques, you are off to a great start.

If you're new to the kitchen, welcome to your new playground!

I hope each encounter with challah baking brings you much joy, satisfaction, and meaning, both in the creation of the challah, the separation and blessings on the challah, and finally in the serving and eating of the challah. There is inspiration to be found in every step of the process.

A NOTE TO PARENTS AND OLDER TWEENS AND TEENS:
Many of the recipes in this book are made with a classic or water challah dough.
They usually require only one piece of dough, approximately the amount of dough you
would use for a medium challah. So, if you're making a big batch of challah dough for Shabbat anyways,
just take off about 32 ounces (about one-eighth of the total dough)
and see what magic can be created with it!

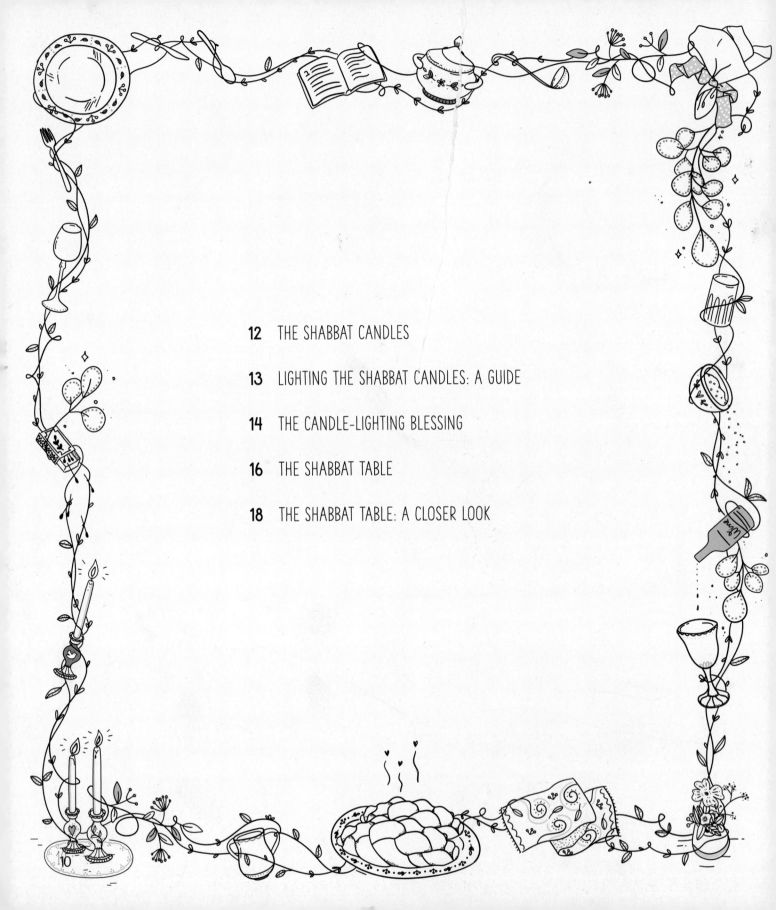

THE SHABBAT CANDLES & TABLESCAPE

SETTING THE SCENE

THE SHABBAT CANDLES

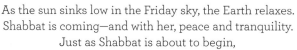

As the sun sinks low in the Friday sky, the Earth relaxes.
Shabbat is coming—and with her, peace and tranquility.
Just as Shabbat is about to begin,
we welcome the Shabbat Queen with candles.
These candles illuminate the home with a magical glow, creating an aura of Shabbat
around the Shabbat table and throughout the entire abode.

Our Sages tell us, *"A little light dispels much darkness."*
When a room is completely dark, one small flame will illuminate the entire space.

Each one of our flames that we kindle for Shabbat introduces a little more light and hope into this world.
Around the Earth, as each woman and girl ignites match to flame, and flame to candle, the lights combine to
create a great sphere of brightness, illuminating the world with the awareness of Shabbat,
and the Oneness of Hashem, bringing peace and tranquility to all of creation.

Our mothers and grandmothers and great-great-great grandmothers have been lighting Shabbat candles for
thousands of years. We are told that even Sarah, Rivkah, Rachel, and Leah, the mothers of the Jewish nation, all lit
candles to welcome Shabbat.

When we light the Shabbat candles, we are a link in this great tradition of women who brought the light of
Shabbat into their homes and made their homes into a place of holiness, warmth, and goodness.

The *Kohen Gadol*, the High Priest of our Holy Temple, the *Beit Hamikdash*,
would kindle the flames of the menorah to bring holiness and light into the world. We do the same with our
Shabbat candles in our homes, our mini Beit Hamikdash.

*THERE IS AN ANCIENT JEWISH CUSTOM, REAWAKENED IN MODERN TIMES BY THE LUBAVITCHER REBBE,
FOR UNMARRIED GIRLS TO LIGHT THEIR OWN SHABBAT (AND HOLIDAY) CANDLE EVERY WEEK FROM THE TIME THEY ARE
ABLE TO UNDERSTAND THE BASIC CONCEPT OF THE MITZVAH AND RECITE THE BLESSING.
FOR THOSE WHO KEEP THIS TRADITION, IT IS CUSTOMARY TO INTRODUCE THIS MITZVAH TO A GIRL BY HER THIRD
BIRTHDAY, THE AGE WHEN CHINUCH, FORMAL JEWISH EDUCATION, BEGINS.

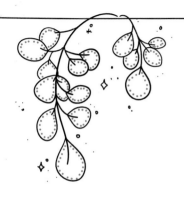

LIGHTING THE SHABBAT CANDLES
A GUIDE

WHEN DO WE LIGHT?

Shabbat candles are lit 18 minutes before sunset on Friday. There are many ways to figure out when this time is, but the easiest way is to go online and search for the Shabbat candle-lighting time in your area that week.

Shabbat candles need to be lit before sunset, because once the sun sets, Shabbat begins and we're not allowed to light a fire on Shabbat.

Candles are also lit to welcome in every Jewish holiday that is mentioned in the Torah. These include Rosh Hashanah, Yom Kippur, Sukkot, Shemini Atzeret/Simchat Torah, Pesach, and Shavuot.

These holidays are very similar to Shabbat in observance. However, unlike Shabbat, we are allowed to use fire to light candles or to cook,* as long as the flame was lit before the holiday began. So, the holiday candles can be lit later in the evening if desired. On the second night of a holiday or when a holiday begins on Saturday night, the candles may only be kindled after nightfall (from a pre-existing flame).

Please visit Chabad.org for the special candle-lighting blessings for each of the holidays, as well as further instructions and information.

WHERE SHOULD WE LIGHT?

The candles are lit to beautify the home for Shabbat, and especially the Shabbat dinner on Friday night. The best place to light them is where we can see them during our Shabbat dinner, and they can give us that special glow that will illuminate our Shabbat meal.

WHAT DO WE LIGHT?

We can light pretty much anything that will stay lit for long enough to light up our Shabbat dinner, and beautify our home. Some have the tradition to light olive oil lamps with wicks, some use regular candles, some like to use colorful ones. Which kind of candle do you choose to light?

WHO LIGHTS?

All Jewish women and and some have the tradition for girls over the age of three to light as well. Girls should light before their mothers, so their mothers can assist them if needed.

It is the special privilege of the women and girls in the home to create this magical atmosphere which brings a special enjoyment to Shabbat and peace in the home.

If there are no women in the home who are able to light the Shabbat candles, the man of the house should light them instead.

PREPARING TO LIGHT

The time of Shabbat candle lighting is so powerful and holy, we like to prepare for it by giving *tzedakah*, charity, to open our hearts to others, and open the channels of blessing. Many people like to keep a special tzedakah box near their candles for this purpose.

HOW ARE THE CANDLES LIT?

Married women light two candles. Many women have the custom to light an additional candle for each of their children.

Unmarried women and girls light one candle, in preparation for the day that they will create the environment of Shabbat in their very own homes.

Wave your arms and hands inward in a circular motion three times, then cover your eyes with your hands, and recite the special blessing on the following page.
This is a powerful time for prayer, take your time.
Uncover your eyes.
It is now Shabbat. *Shabbat Shalom!*

Except for the holiday of Yom Kippur, during which all the laws of Shabbat apply, including those of fire, whatever day of the week it is.

THE CANDLE-LIGHTING BLESSING

Light the candles and then stretch your hands out towards the lit flames.
Draw them inwards towards you in a circular motion three times, welcoming the Shabbat Queen into your life, into your home, and into the world. After the third time, cover your eyes with your hands and recite the following blessing*:

בָּרוּךְ אַתָּה יי אֱ-לֹהֵינוּ מֶלֶךְ הָעוֹלָם
אֲשֶׁר קִדְּשָׁנוּ בְּמִצְוֹתָיו וְצִוָּנוּ לְהַדְלִיק נֵר שֶׁל שַׁבָּת (קֹדֶשׁ).

*Ba-ruch A-tah A-do-nai E-lo-heinu Me-lech ha-o-lam
a-sher ki-de-sha-nu b'mitz-vo-tav v'tzi-va-nu l'hadlik ner shel Shabbat (ko-desh**).*

**You, Ado-nai, the Source of blessings,
our G-d, Master of the universe, has made us holy with His mitzvot
and instructed us to kindle the light of the (holy) Shabbat.**

This is a precious and powerful moment of light and prayer. Throughout the ages, Jewish women, secure behind the veil of their hands, have relied on this prayerful time to communicate the deepest desires of their hearts. Some pray in their own words, and some recite this prayer. They ask for the blessing of creating a home filled with the Divine presence, and the merit to raise children and grandchildren, wise and upright generations living in the light of Hashem's love, and illuminating the world with Torah and their beautiful deeds. In the merit of our first mothers, Sarah, Rivkah, Rachel, and Leah, may our candles burn bright and forever, amen.

יְהִי רָצוֹן מִלְּפָנֶיךָ ה' אֱלֹקַי וֵאלֹקֵי אֲבוֹתַי, שֶׁתְּחוֹנֵן אוֹתִי (וְאֶת אִישִׁי וְאֶת בָּנַי וְאֶת אָבִי וְאֶת אִמִּי) וְאֶת כָּל קְרוֹבַי, וְתִתֵּן לָנוּ וּלְכָל יִשְׂרָאֵל חַיִּים טוֹבִים וַאֲרוּכִים, וְתִזְכְּרֵנוּ בְּזִכְרוֹן טוֹבָה וּבְרָכָה, וְתִפְקְדֵנוּ בִּפְקֻדַּת יְשׁוּעָה וְרַחֲמִים, וּתְבָרְכֵנוּ בְּרָכוֹת גְּדוֹלוֹת, וְתַשְׁלִים בָּתֵּינוּ וְתַשְׁכֵּן שְׁכִינָתְךָ בֵּינֵינוּ, וְזַכֵּנוּ לְגַדֵּל בָּנִים וּבְנֵי בָנִים חֲכָמִים וּנְבוֹנִים אוֹהֲבֵי ה', יִרְאֵי אֱלֹקִים אַנְשֵׁי אֱמֶת זֶרַע קֹדֶשׁ, בַּה' דְּבֵקִים, וּמְאִירִים אֶת הָעוֹלָם בַּתּוֹרָה וּבְמַעֲשִׂים טוֹבִים וּבְכָל מְלֶאכֶת עֲבוֹדַת הַבּוֹרֵא, אָנָּא, שְׁמַע אֶת תְּחִנָּתִי בָּעֵת הַזֹּאת בִּזְכוּת שָׂרָה וְרִבְקָה רָחֵל וְלֵאָה אִמּוֹתֵינוּ, וְהָאֵר נֵרֵנוּ שֶׁלֹּא יִכְבֶּה לְעוֹלָם וָעֶד, וְהָאֵר פָּנֶיךָ וְנִוָּשֵׁעָה, אָמֵן.

Uncover your eyes, it's Shabbat now.
Shabbat Shalom!

** This blessing is specific to Shabbat.
Please search your prayerbook or Chabad.org for the blessings
to recite when lighting holiday candles.*

** some have the tradition to add the word kodesh, which means holy.

THIS PAGE IS DEDICATED IN HONOR OF RIVKAH ORLI BAT SARAH.
A true Eishet Chayil, she leads her family with dignity and strength, illuminating her home, and the world, with her kindness.

Setting the Scene
THE SHABBAT TABLE

THERE ARE TWO ANGELS WHO COME INTO OUR HOME ON FRIDAY NIGHT.

ONE IS A GOOD ANGEL. THE OTHER JUST WANTS TO MAKE TROUBLE.

WHEN THEY COME INSIDE, IF THEY FIND THE SHABBAT CANDLES LIT AND THE TABLE BEAUTIFULLY SET,

THE GOOD ANGEL SMILES AND SAYS,

"MAY IT BE G-D'S WILL THAT NEXT SHABBAT BE THE SAME,"

AND THE TROUBLEMAKING ANGEL HAS NO CHOICE BUT TO ANSWER, "AMEN!"

Shabbat 119b

16

nce upon a time, in the Land of Israel, in the city of Jerusalem, high, high up on a hill, there was a beautiful temple.

It was called the *Beit Hamikdash*, the Sacred House, and it was the holiest place in the whole world. Standing tall and majestic on the mountain, it glistened with golden objects and magnificent draperies. Inside, there were many special items, each beautiful and each with its own unique meaning and purpose. But the most wondrous part of the *Beit Hamikdash* was that it was filled with Hashem's presence.

The Divine presence, the *Shechinah* Herself, rested in this house and made everything within it alive and miraculous.

We don't have the *Beit Hamikdash* anymore, although we pray every day for it to be rebuilt soon. But we do have something else: our own homes. When we were told to build the *Beit Hamikdash*, Hashem said to us, "Build for Me a temple and I will dwell within them." *"Them" means us!* It means that we—each of us—can turn ourselves and our homes into a miraculous Temple where Hashem's presence is felt and welcomed.

How do we transform an ordinary house into a miniature *Beit Hamikdash*? By using everything in the home for holy purposes. Wine becomes *Kiddush*. Bread becomes *Challah*. When we use our dining room table as a Shabbat table, it's no longer just a table—it is an altar, just like the *mizbeyach* in the *Beit Hamikdash*. And the challah we place upon it is like a *korban*, an offering that was brought in Temple times.

Let's take a look at how we set the Shabbat table, and how everything we put on it has its own holy meaning and purpose.

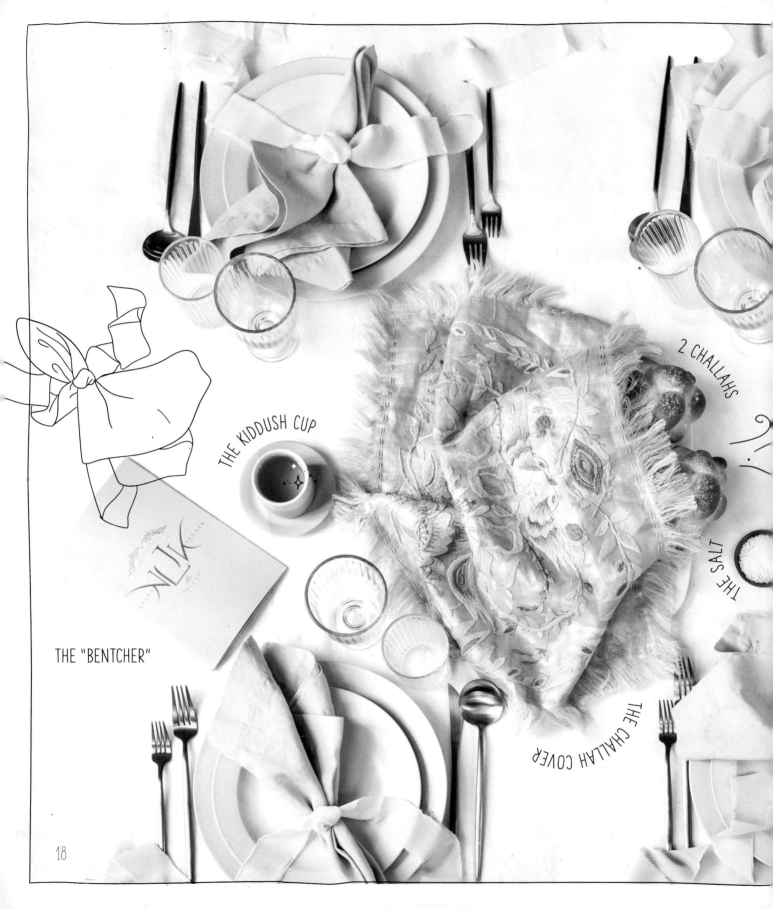

2 CHALLAHS

THE KIDDUSH CUP

THE SALT

THE "BENTCHER"

THE CHALLAH COVER

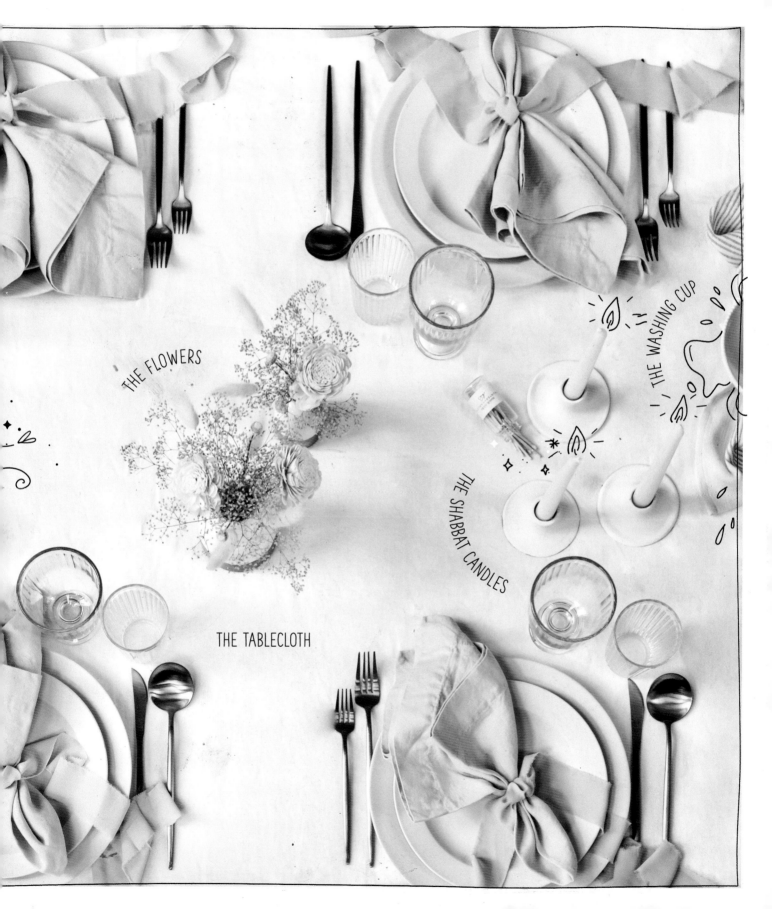

THE FLOWERS

THE WASHING CUP

THE SHABBAT CANDLES

THE TABLECLOTH

THE SHABBAT TABLE
A Closer Look

THE TABLE

The altar in the Temple is called *"the table that is placed before Hashem"* (Ezekiel 41:22).

When we had the *Beit Hamikdash*, we would bring sacrifices on the altar to help us become better people, and to ask forgiveness. Now that we have no *Beit Hamikdash*, our table—which we use to feed the hungry and gather friends and family in peace and harmony—becomes a way for us to become better through giving to others.

THE TABLECLOTH

There's a special tradition to cover our table with a tablecloth in honor of Shabbat to show respect for this holy day. Some people have a tradition that the tablecloth should be white to remind us of the white *manna*. The Shabbat tablecloth also reminds us of the layer of dew that covered the desert ground before the *manna* fell, serving as a layer of protection for this special food. (When we wandered in the desert after being redeemed from our slavery in Egypt, the *manna* fell every single day for 40 years. It was the most perfect food to nourish us, just like mother's milk.)

THE BEAUTIFUL TABLE SETTING*

Setting the Shabbat table is a special job. We are being visited by a queen, the Shabbat Queen herself.

As we would for any royal visit, we put out our nicest dishes, glasses, and silverware, and even a bouquet of flowers to make it extra special.

THE SHABBAT CANDLES

In the *Beit Hamikdash* there was a *menorah*, a special seven-branched candelabra. It was lit every morning and filled the *Beit Hamikdash* with special holy light. The candles we kindle for Shabbat also provide us with a special light, and make our home feel beautiful, holy, and illuminated. They don't have to be on the Shabbat table, but they should be close by. We want to enjoy our Shabbat dinner by their light.

THE KIDDUSH CUP

Wine is a special drink. It can make people act silly, but it can also make people happy and is often used at celebrations. When someone makes a toast at a wedding or any special event, they usually hold up a cup of wine and say *l'chaim*.

We have a special *mitzvah* to remember Shabbat—not just in our minds but with our words. For that, we need to lift a glass.

When we recite the special *Kiddush* blessing while holding a cup of wine (or grape juice), we are using the wine for a holy purpose and correcting all the times wine was used the wrong way.

20

The lovely napkins, tablecloths, silverware, and other items of beauty found on the table on the previous spread were generously loaned by Eve Singer @Broyt.

Kiddush wine also reminds us of the wine that was poured on the altar in the *Beit Hamikdash*, with each offering that was brought.

THE WASH CUP

In the *Beit Hamikdash* there was a *kiyor*, a wash basin, where the priests would wash their hands and feet before beginning their service. Similarly, we wash our hands before eating challah (or any bread or matzah) as an act of purification.

THE CHALLAH

We set two challahs on the Shabbat table (even if we will only end up eating one), like the double portion of *manna* that fell every Friday in the desert to sustain us through Shabbat. This reminds us that even if our food isn't falling directly from the heavens today, it is always a gift from Hashem. We trust that even if we don't work on Shabbat, Hashem will provide for all of our needs and we will not go hungry.

Another significance of the two challahs: In the *Beit Hamikdash* there was a special table that always had 12 loaves of unique and holy bread on it, called the *lechem hapanim*, each representing one of the 12 tribes of Israel. Some people have a custom of braiding their two challahs with a total of 12 strands, or setting 12 challahs on their Shabbat table, reminding us of the 12 tribes, and that we are all united as one.

THE CHALLAH COVER*

We keep our challahs covered with a special cloth until it is time to eat them. This cover reminds us of the layer of dew that fell on top of the *manna* in the desert. (The tablecloth represents the bottom layer and the challah cover represents the top layer.)

THE SALT

Our table is like the *mizbeyach*, the altar, in the *Beit Hamikdash*—the food we put on it—our offering. Every offering in the *Beit Hamikdash* needed to have salt added to it. Similarly, before we eat the challah we make sure to dip it into salt. Salt is harsh and challah is sweet. We always want the sweet to overpower the harsh, so we make sure to dip the challah into the salt instead of pouring the salt over the challah.

THE "BENTCHER," OR "BIRKON"

We recite blessings before partaking of the wine and challah, just as we do before partaking of any food or drink. We must also remember to thank Hashem after we finish enjoying the delicious meal full of the good foods He created. "*Bentch*" is the Yiddish word for "bless." "*Birkon*" is the Hebrew word for "a booklet of blessings." Having a booklet of the prayers and blessings helps us know what to say and reminds us not to leave the table without saying, "Thank You!"

The magnificent challah covers you'll see throughout this book were graciously loaned by Micaela Ezra of Ahyin Judaica.

EVERYTHING YOU NEVER KNEW YOU KNEADED

THE MAGIC OF CHALLAH

WHAT IS CHALLAH?

"Wait... is this a trick question?"

Of course you know what challah is—that's why you got this book! (Smart move, by the way.)

"Okay, seriously, who doesn't know about challah?"
It's a soft, pillowy, delicious bread we eat on Shabbat and holidays. It's usually braided into a beautiful shape, and often is pretty sweet too.

Ya... but did you ever wonder why it's not just called Shabbat bread?

What makes it challah anyway—is it the shape?

If we don't braid it, is it still called challah?

Where does the word "challah" even come from?

Have I gotten you curious yet?

Let's dive right into that challah bowl for some answers!

The word "challah" comes straight from the Torah. Hashem (G-d) gives us a special *mitzvah*, a Divine instruction, to remove a portion of every batch of dough we prepare and give it to Him as a gift. This portion of dough is called *challah*.

How are we supposed to give our dough to Hashem?

Well, in the ancient days, when we all lived in the Holy Land of Israel, we would give it to the *kohanim*, the priests. They worked for Hashem in the *Beit Hamikdash*

and this was one of the gifts we gave them for their holy service. After the *Beit Hamikdash* was destroyed, our Sages instructed us to continue to take off the piece of dough, the *challah* gift, and to burn it. This would serve as a reminder that all of our food, and indeed all of our blessings, are gifts from Above.

The mitzvah of *challah* is here to remind us that we don't control what or how much we get in this life. We do our part to bring the blessings into our life, but Hashem is the One in charge, and all our gifts really come from Him.

So, *challah* is a gift! It reminds us where all our gifts come from, and that's why we call our Shabbat bread 'challah.'

Shabbat is the day we rest from creating, just as Hashem rested on the seventh day of creation. It's a day we rest from making stuff happen. We don't build, we don't destroy, we don't change things, and we don't travel to other places. We just appreciate the world, and where we are in it, as it is right now.

On Shabbat we say "thank you" to Hashem for all of our gifts, and remember that we can just be, and we don't always have to do.

Sometimes we get so caught up in the "business" of life, that we forget who we really are. We start to think of ourselves as a child, a teen, an adult, a sibling, a friend, a competitor, a student, short, tall, curly haired, athletic, bookish, shy, brave ... so many labels!

And with all those labels, maybe we forget that deep inside we are a pure and holy *neshamah*, a soul. A soul that is a breath of Hashem, a soul that gives us life and is perfect just the way it is.

Yes. You—regardless of what you may do or not do, however you may look or think or feel—are a perfect, holy, and precious gift from Hashem.

This is the message of Shabbat and this is the message of the challah we make and serve to celebrate it. That it is possible for us to do all the stuff we need to do, and then to take a step back and remember who we really are. And that is a gift.

The mitzvah of *challah* and the day of Shabbat both remind us that who we are and all we have come from Hashem.

Whatever type of bread we serve on our Shabbat (or holiday) table can be called challah. But we don't want to serve just any ordinary bread on such a special day! We make a dough that is sweet and rich, and maybe even add in some unique and delicious flavors. After separating the little piece of "*challah*" to burn, we braid or shape the dough in special ways to make it beautiful and then we bake it (wait 'til you see some of the wild shapes and recipes in this book!).

Then we place the challah bread on our Shabbat table and remind ourselves that Hashem is taking care of us. And so, we can sniff deeply, inhale the incredible aroma of the freshly baked challah, and relax.

There is a blessing we recite before eating the challah, and before each time we eat bread during the week as well. Here's how it goes:

"Baruch Atah Ado-nai Elo-heinu Melech ha-olam hamotzi lechem min ha-aretz."

In English these words mean, "You, Hashem, our G-d, King of the Universe, are the Source of all blessings and have caused the earth to bring forth bread."

Yes, another reminder that everything—even our bread—is from Hashem.

And then … yum! We take a big chomp out of that challah and feel the joy of Shabbat in every bite.

Turn to page 27 for step-by-step instructions on how to separate a portion of your dough as challah.
Turn to page 28 for many more details about the mitzvah of separating challah dough.

THE TRADITIONS & LAWS OF CHALLAH

CHALLAH TODAY & THROUGHOUT THE AGES

A GUIDE TO
הפרשת חלה
SEPARATING THE CHALLAH

WHAT COUNTS AS A DOUGH THAT REQUIRES CHALLAH SEPARATION?

1. The dough needs to be made from one or more of the five grains listed in the Torah as "bread" grains, upon which the blessing of *hamotzi* is recited. These are wheat, barley, oat, spelt, and rye.

2. In order to be able to recite the challah separation blessing, the majority of the recipe's liquid content must be water. If the majority of the liquid is not water (i.e., honey, oil, eggs, milk, juice, etc.), so long as there is even one drop of water in the dough, the challah portion is separated but the blessing is not recited.

3. The dough needs to have a certain amount of flour.

   - A dough that uses less than 2 lb. 11 oz. (1230 grams) of flour does not require any challah separation.

   - A dough that uses between 2 lb. 11 oz. and 3 lb. 11 oz of flour requires challah separation, but the blessing is not recited. *Most of the recipes in this book are in this category.*

   - A dough that uses over 3 lb. 11 oz. of flour requires a separation of challah and the blessing is recited.

WHEN DO WE SEPARATE CHALLAH?

We separate challah from a dough that has already been kneaded and risen. Let out the extra air and you're ready.

WHO MAY SEPARATE CHALLAH?

The *mitzvah* of *hafrashat* (separating) *challah* is for any Jew over the age of bar or bat mitzvah. However, this mitzvah is one of the special *mitzvot* of the woman, and therefore, even if a guy made the dough, a woman should be the one to recite the blessing if possible. If there is no woman available to do the *mitzvah*, a man (or boy over 13) should do it himself.

WHAT DO WE DO WITH THE PIECE OF DOUGH WE SEPARATE?

This piece of dough, called "*challah*," is sacred. We are not allowed to eat it or to feed it to anyone, not even our pets! The best way to make sure that nobody will eat it is to burn it until it is inedible.

To burn the piece of dough, make sure that nothing else is in the oven at the same time and burn it until it's charcoal black. I like to pop it into my toaster oven that is set to broil; it gets burnt nice and quickly that way. Some people like to burn it directly on their stovetop. Other people save it in the freezer until they finally burn it with all the *chametz* right before Pesach.

However you choose to burn it, once it's fully burnt, it can be discarded.

(If it's not possible to burn the challah, some are of the opinion that it's okay to wrap it up very well and throw it away even without burning. But all agree that burning it is the preferred method.)

WHAT IF I'M MAKING A BUNCH OF DIFFERENT SMALL DOUGHS?

Sometimes you'll want to make a few different recipes, and while each one may be too small to do the separation or make the challah blessing, together they are a big enough portion for the mitzvah.

In that case, you may combine the doughs by covering them all with the same towel and then reciting the challah blessing on them all together.

OOPS. WHAT IF I FORGOT TO SEPARATE THE DOUGH AND ALREADY BAKED THE CHALLAH?

If a person forgets to separate challah before baking the dough, challah may (and should) still be separated after baking.

Combine all the baked challahs in a container or cover them all together with one towel. Remove a small piece from one of the loaves. Recite the blessing as usual (if the dough was large enough to qualify).

If on Shabbat you realize that the challah portion was accidentally not separated, the challah loaf may still be eaten on Shabbat, as long as this happened outside of the Land of Israel. A slice of the challah loaf should be set aside in a safe spot where it will not be eaten. After Shabbat, challah will need to be separated from this slice. The slice should be large enough that even after the piece of challah is removed there will still be enough left over to eat.

There's lots more to know about separating challah!
For more in-depth information, please see my first challah cookbook, RISING! The Book of Challah. *For a complete overview of the laws of challah separation, please see* Kitzur Shulchan Aruch, *Chapter 35.*

CHALLAH TRADITIONS & CUSTOMS

Challah is served on Shabbat and holidays and at every "simchah," or special occasion. Whenever something special is happening, you know there will be challah! Because of its importance, both the mitzvah of the separation of the piece of 'challah' and the serving of the baked loaves of challah, many traditions have been established in the way we serve the challah and the way we eat the challah. Here are some of the special challah traditions and customs that have developed over the thousands of years of challah baking and serving.

BRAIDING & SHAPING CHALLAH

Originally, challahs weren't braided at all. They were very basic shapes, like the pitas or laffahs of the Middle East. But starting in 15th century Germany, and then later in Eastern Europe, Jewish women started to braid them into lots of pretty shapes, and challahs started to become more sweet and richer as well.

Braiding challah is a way to make it look more beautiful and special than the regular bread we eat every day, and is a way to show that this is a bread for a holy occasion.

Some of the shaping and braiding traditions started because of different challah practices that made braiding the challahs both practical and meaningful.

One of the reasons braiding challah became popular is because of the custom to tear the challah rather than cut it with a knife (see "Cutting the Challah" on page 30).

Tearing a big loaf of bread with your hands is hard work! When a challah is braided, it becomes really easy to tear off pieces and give them to all the people who are eagerly awaiting theirs.

The most traditional challah shape is the six-strand braid. Since we serve two challahs at the Shabbat meal, this gives us a total of 12 strands, which connects us to a Kabbalistic idea of having 12 loaves or strands on our Shabbat table.[1]

---

1 «The Arizal (Rabbi Yitzchak Luria Ashkenazi, 1534–1572, Torah scholar and Kabbalist, based in Safed, Israel), in his poem "*Azamer Bishvachin*," traditionally sung at the Shabbat table on Friday nights, writes, "*Shechinta titatar beshit nahamei listar*" (May the *Shechinah*, the Divine presence, be adorned by the six strands on each side).

These 12 loaves or strands remind us of the 12 loaves of bread that were always present in the *Beit Hamikdash*, each loaf representing another tribe of Israel. When we have 12 loaves or strands at our meal, it's like we are recreating the unity of all the 12 tribes of Israel. This unity brings the *Shechinah*, the Divine presence, to rest upon our Shabbat table.

Another beautiful explanation of the six-strand challah is that it represents the six days of the work-week—days of separateness and division—all coming together to form a perfect whole, the day of Shabbat.

Round Challahs: A well-established practice is that of the round or spiral challah that is used on Rosh Hashanah and throughout the entire month of Tishrei, in which the New Year and High Holidays are celebrated.

The round shape signifies the cycle of life. Just as in a circle there is no set start point or end point, so too in life, every moment can be utilized as a "start-over" moment; we are always given the opportunity to turn a new leaf and start fresh.

Another way to interpret the spiral challah shape is that it represents the passage of time. Even though time goes in circles and cycles, and we celebrate the same holidays every year over again, each time we come back around the sun, we are changed. We have used the opportunities of each holiday and season to grow and evolve. When we come back to the same holiday, we are more than what we were last time we experienced this season, just like the spiral, which circles 'round and 'round, but grows with each cycle.

Some of the challah shapes in this book that are ancient traditions are the "Bird on Spiral Challah" for the meal before Yom Kippur (page 243), and the "Hand Challah" for Hoshana Raba (page 245).

There are many other traditions of challah shapes for the various holidays that I have shown you in this book, along with some new and original ideas …. Maybe we'll start some new challah traditions together!

SPECIAL CHALLAH PRAYERS

According to the Ben Ish Chai, the woman of the house says the following verse when she places the challahs on the Shabbat table: *"Zeh ha-shulchan asher lifnei Hashem"* [This is the table that is before G-d]" (Ezekiel 41:22).

It is also traditional to recite the words, *"L'kavod Shabbat kodesh"* (in honor the holy Shabbat), throughout the preparing, kneading, and braiding of the challah dough. This helps the baker keep his or her intentions pure and focused throughout the process.

SERVING THE CHALLAH

There are a number of traditions regarding how the challah is to be served after it has been cut. Some throw a slice to each person sitting around the table, while others pass it around on a platter. There are those who place the sliced challah in the center of the table for each person to take on their own. Many are careful not to place the challah directly into a person's hands.

The Sephardic interpretation of throwing the challah towards a person is that it represents a downpour of wealth and sustenance. The Ashkenazi explanation for this custom is that handing another person bread is like giving him a "handout" and shows that the person is impoverished or needy. Either way, both reasons signify bounty and blessing.

CHALLAH AND SALT

Our home is our temple, and our table is the altar. On the altar in the Beit Hamikdash there was always salt. So too, we make sure to keep salt on our table during each meal where bread is served.

The custom is to dip the challah or bread into salt before eating the first bite. Many communities have the tradition to dip their challah or bread into the salt three times before partaking of it.[2]

---

2 The word *melach* (salt) is the word *lechem* (bread) in reverse. The numerical value of both those words is 78, which is three times 26, the numerical value of Hashem's holy name that represents *chesed*, pure giving. When we dip *"lechem"* into *"melach"* three times, we are drawing in more chesed and sweetening judgments. Also, the numerical value of the word *mazlah* (the *mazal*) equals 78. By dipping the bread into salt, we are symbolically bringing good *mazal* (fortune) into our lives.

CUTTING THE CHALLAH

No knives or weapons of any kind were permitted upon the altar in the Beit Hamikdash. Since our tables are compared to the altar, many people are careful to not put a knife to their challah and to tear it instead.

However, there is another well-known custom to mark the challah that will be eaten first. This is done by using a knife to make a small slit on the surface of the challah.

COVERING THE CHALLAH

Across all communities and traditions, there is a custom to cover the challah on the Shabbat table before kiddush is recited.

One reason for this is that we are making the blessing over the wine before the blessing on the bread. Usually bread is the food we make the first blessing on, as it is the most important, however since we say the blessing on the wine first on Shabbat, we cover the challah so it won't be embarrassed. This teaches us an important lesson in sensitivity towards others. If we are so careful with the feelings of our challah, how much more careful we must be with the feelings of all the people around our Shabbat table.

Another reason given for the covering of the challah is that the challah represents the manna, which was always protected with a layer of dew underneath it and a layer of dew above it. The tablecloth (or challah board) under the challah, and the challah cover above it, protect our challah in the same way.

DISPOSING OF CHALLAH

This is unlikely to happen! Your challah will be so delicious, there won't be a drop left. If there is any leftover, there are so many wonderful ideas in this book for what you can do with it, you'll never need to throw away any challah again.

That said, sometimes there are a few pieces that need to be thrown away. Since challah is so special, we want to be sensitive in how we do this.

Some communities won't throw out even a crumb of challah. If there is any leftover challah, they will feed it to the birds. Others will throw away extra challah, but in a respectful manner. They will either break it up into very small pieces or wrap it in some sort of covering before disposing of it.

CHALLAH AS A BLESSING

The moment of challah separation is an opportune time for us to pray for all that we need and desire in our lives and in the lives of others. Additionally, our Sages have told us that the mitzvah of hafrashat challah brings many blessings. Here are some:

☆ **AN EASY AND SAFE BIRTH.** For this reason, it is customary for a woman to separate challah at least once in her ninth month of pregnancy.

☆ **HEALING AND WHOLENESS.** Challah is the bread of healing. The numeric value of the word challah is 43, which is the same as the Hebrew word for inclusion, "*gam.*" It is a *segulah* (positive omen) to pray for health and for the wholeness we seek, in ourselves and others, whether it is to find a soulmate, have a child, or achieve physical, emotional, spiritual, or mental healing.

☆ **FINANCIAL SECURITY AND PROSPERITY.** According to our Sages, the mitzvah of separating challah brings a blessing of wealth into the home. In 15th-century Germany, the name for challah was "*berches,*" which comes from the verse, "*Birkat Hashem hee taasheer,*" Hashem's blessings bring riches (Mishlei 10:22).

☆ **TESHUVAH.** Challah is a special segulah for *teshuvah*, returning to our true self, and reconnecting with Hashem. It is recommended that a person should do the mitzvah of *hafrashat challah* at least once a year. Ideally, this mitzvah should be done in the 10 days of teshuvah between Rosh Hashanah and Yom Kippur.

THE CHALLAH BLESSING AND PRAYER

This page is dedicated in honor of Sarah Fenna bat Rivka (Reifschneider Korn)
May you see the realization of the blessing of the Shabbat lights, and merit to raise, beautiful, wise, and upstanding generations.

THE CHALLAH BLESSING

*Please see page 27 to learn all about this mitzvah
and how it should be practiced.*

Recite this blessing with deep intention. This is your moment to reconnect.
Visualize your soul, your *neshamah*, infinite and eternal, reconnecting to its Source,
the Infinite and Transcendent light of Hashem,
wherein all is possible and all blessings and goodness already exist.
Draw the blessings down from this space of everything
into your dough and into all of your life.

בָּרוּךְ אַתָּה יי אֱ־לֹהֵינוּ מֶלֶךְ הָעוֹלָם
אֲשֶׁר קִדְּשָׁנוּ בְּמִצְוֹתָיו וְצִוָּנוּ לְהַפְרִישׁ חַלָּה
(מִן הָעִסָה).

*Ba-ruch A-tah A-do-nai Elo-heinu Me-lech ha-o-lam a-sher kid-sha-nu b'mitz-vo-tav
v'tzi-va-nu l'haf-rish challah (some add: min ha-i-sah).*

You, Ado-nai, the Source of all blessings, our G-d, Master of the universe,
has made us holy with His mitzvot and instructed us to separate challah
(some add: from the dough).

Then, remove a small piece—approximately one ounce—from the dough.
Immediately after separating it, hold the piece of dough aloft and say:

הֲרֵי זוּ חַלָּה.

Ha-rei zu challah.

Behold, this is Challah.

Now, burn the dough or dispose of it appropriately.
See page 27 for detailed instructions.

THE CHALLAH PRAYER

Some people have the tradition of reciting the traditional
"Yehi Ratzon" prayer below following the challah separation.
Whether you say these particular passages, or just say words from your heart,
this moment is yours for prayer.

יְהִי רָצוֹן מִלְּפָנֶיךָ יְיָ אֱלֹהֵינוּ וֵאלֹהֵי אֲבוֹתֵינוּ שֶׁהַמִּצְוָה שֶׁל הַפְרָשַׁת חַלָּה תֵּחָשֵׁב כְּאִלּוּ קִיַּמְתִּיהָ בְּכָל
פְּרָטֶיהָ וְדִקְדּוּקֶיהָ, וְתֵחָשֵׁב הֲרָמַת הַחַלָּה שֶׁאֲנִי מְרִימָה, כְּמוֹ הַקָּרְבָּן שֶׁהָקְרַב עַל הַמִּזְבֵּחַ, שֶׁנִּתְקַבֵּל
בְּרָצוֹן. וּכְמוֹ שֶׁלְּפָנִים הָיְתָה הַחַלָּה נְתוּנָה לַכֹּהֵן וְהָיְתָה זוֹ לְכַפָּרַת עֲוֹנוֹת, כָּךְ תִּהְיֶה לְכַפָּרָה לַעֲוֹנוֹתַי,
וְאָז אֶהְיֶה כְּאִלּוּ נוֹלַדְתִּי מֵחָדָשׁ, נְקִיָּה מֵחֵטְא וְעָוֹן. וְאוּכַל לְקַיֵּם מִצְוַת שַׁבָּת קֹדֶשׁ וְהַיָּמִים הַטּוֹבִים עִם
בַּעֲלִי (וִילָדֵינוּ), לִהְיוֹת נִזוֹנִים מִקְּדֻשַּׁת הַיָּמִים הָאֵלֶּה. וּמֵהַשְׁפָּעַתָהּ שֶׁל מִצְוַת חַלָּה, יִהְיוּ יְלָדֵינוּ נִזוֹנִים
תָּמִיד מִיָּדָיו שֶׁל הַקָּדוֹשׁ בָּרוּךְ הוּא, בְּרֹב רַחֲמָיו וַחֲסָדָיו, וּבְרֹב אַהֲבָה, וְשֶׁתִּתְקַבֵּל מִצְוַת חַלָּה כְּאִלּוּ
נָתַתִּי מַעֲשֵׂר. וּכְשֵׁם שֶׁהִנְנִי מְקַיֶּמֶת מִצְוַת חַלָּה בְּכָל לֵב, כָּךְ יִתְעוֹרְרוּ רַחֲמָיו שֶׁל הַקָּדוֹשׁ בָּרוּךְ הוּא
לְשָׁמְרֵנִי מִצַּעַר וּמִמַּכְאוֹבִים כָּל הַיָּמִים, אָמֵן.

May it be Your will, Creator, Source of all life and blessing,
that the challah separation I perform this day,
be pure in its deed and intention.
May the elevation of this challah gift be considered
the truest offering of my heart.
Just as the giving of challah to the kohen in Temple times served as an atonement
for the individual, so may this offering serve to renew and awaken me, and to
reconnect me to Your light.
May the gift of challah empower me and my loved ones to find joy and meaning in
the oasis that is Shabbat, and to be imbued and sustained
with its holiness throughout the week.
May the spiritual influence of this challah gift build a home and a family
that is centered on loving-kindness and is continuously nurtured and supported
by the light of the Infinite. And just as I offer this challah gift with the fullness of
my heart, so may the heart of the Divine Presence be aroused to
compassion and keep me, my family and all the universe,
free from sorrow and pain, always, *amen*.

THE INGREDIENTS

THERE ARE SEVEN INGREDIENTS IN A CLASSIC CHALLAH,
LIKE THE SIX DAYS OF CREATION THAT BROUGHT THE WORLD TO LIFE, PLUS SHABBAT!
THESE INGREDIENTS ARE A RECIPE FOR CHALLAH
AND ALSO REMIND US OF THE INGREDIENTS FOR A GOOD LIFE.

WITH THESE SEVEN INGREDIENTS OUR CHALLAH WILL RISE.
IF WE ARE SURE TO HAVE ALL THESE INGREDIENTS IN OUR LIVES,
WE WILL ALSO RISE TO BE OUR BEST SELVES.

WATER

FLOUR

We start the challah recipe with water.

Water is like our soul.
It is forever, it is pure, and it is life-giving.

When we search for life on other planets, the first thing we need to find out is whether that planet has water. Where there's water, there's life!

The human body seems quite solid, but did you know that we are mostly water?

This reminds us that when we look into the mirror, we need to see past our body.

Our body is just a house for our true self, the breath of G-d that is our soul. And that soul is who we truly are. It is perfect, it is beautiful, and it can never be ruined.

When we see the beautiful G-dly spark within ourselves, we can also see it in all the people we meet.

Flour is the body of the dough and is like our body.

You can't survive by eating plain flour (yuck!), but if you mix it with water, it becomes alive—just like a body that has a soul.

Since our body is the house for our soul, it is important to keep the body in good shape.

When the house is well taken care of, the soul inside it can shine through.

When we feel good in our body, our thoughts, our words, and the things we do are able to be expressions of our truest and best self.

WHAT KIND OF FLOUR SHOULD I USE?

White, unbleached, "all-purpose" flour is usually perfect for challah. To make it healthier, you can use whole wheat flour or flour made of other grains (such as spelt), and sometimes even a mix of different flours.

When making a challah that has lots of extra stuff in it—like multiple types of flour, seeds, chocolate, etc.—I recommend you use high-gluten or bread flour.

PUTTING THE FLOUR IN

- To measure the flour, simply scoop it into a dry measuring cup. You don't have to pack it down, just fill the cup, and tap it on the counter so the flour settles in.

- When adding flour, always add a little at a time. Too much flour will dry out your dough—and once you've put it in you can't take it out. Try to use as close to the lowest amount of flour in the recipe as possible.

WHAT TEMPERATURE SHOULD THE WATER BE?

The water we use in our challah recipe should be very warm—I call it baby-bath warm. If you would put a baby in that water for her bath, it's perfect for challah.

DID YOU KNOW?

ALL THE WATER ON EARTH TODAY IS THE SAME WATER THAT HAS BEEN ON EARTH SINCE THE BEGINNING OF TIME! THE WATER CYCLES JUST LIKE OUR SOUL, JOURNEYING ON THIS EARTH, GOING BACK TO ITS SOURCE, AND THEN COMING BACK TO EARTH AGAIN.

SUGAR

Sugar helps our challah grow. It also reminds us that when we are sweet and kind to others, we grow to be our best selves. Not just that, we help those people grow to be their best selves too!

Sugar plays a very important role in our challah recipe.

A FEW THINGS THE SUGAR DOES

- ❧ Sugar gives the crust of the challah a golden color.
- ❧ Sugar helps retain moisture in the challah, keeping it soft and squishy—just the way we like it!
- ❧ Sugar makes the challah rise more than it otherwise would.
- ❧ Sugar makes our challah taste different from regular bread, sweeter and more special for Shabbat and holidays.

DID YOU KNOW?

THERE ARE OTHER INGREDIENTS (SOME ARE HEALTHIER THAN SUGAR) THAT YOU CAN PUT INTO CHALLAH TO MAKE IT YUMMY AND SWEET?

HONEY IS A GREAT WAY TO SWEETEN CHALLAH—IT IS EVEN SWEETER THAN SUGAR! AGAVE NECTAR, DATE SYRUP, MOLASSES, AND BROWN SUGAR ARE A FEW OTHER CHOICES.

YEAST

If you mix flour and water together and leave them alone for a while, yeast will come to visit! Yeast spores are always in the air. They will jump right into our challah dough, gobble up the sugars in the flour, as well as all the extra sugar we put into the dough, and turn them into carbon dioxide and alcohol. This will puff up the dough and make it rise.

Waiting for the yeast in the air, also known as wild yeast, to do its thing takes a long time and produces what is known as sourdough.

When we want to make a challah more quickly, the best way to do so is by including ready-made yeast in our recipe. This starts the rising process right away and we don't have to wait around for those yeast spores in the air to come visit.

WHICH YEAST SHOULD I BUY?

You will notice that a few types of yeast are sold in stores. There are fresh yeast cubes in the refrigerator section, and dry yeast granules packed in envelopes, little glass jars, or large bags in the baking aisle. Usually marked as active yeast, instant yeast, or quick (or rapid) rise yeast, these dry yeasts are all very similar and can be used interchangeably with all the recipes in this book.

You can use fresh yeast, but be aware that it spoils relatively quickly. Fresh yeast can last up to two weeks in the fridge and three months in the freezer. I prefer to use dry yeast—I don't see any difference in the flavor of the challah.

CONVERSION CHART IF USING FRESH YEAST:

2 oz. fresh yeast (57 grams) = 7 teaspoons dry yeast
1 packed tablespoon fresh yeast (21 grams) = 2 teaspoons dry yeast

STORING YOUR YEAST:

Fresh yeast must be refrigerated or frozen (but should be used at room temperature).

Once a package of dry yeast is opened, it should be stored in an airtight container in the freezer (for up to six months) or back of the fridge (for up to four months). If you're not sure about the freshness of your yeast, you can try putting a teaspoon of it into some warm water with sugar, and let it sit for a few minutes. If the yeast starts foaming or bubbling, you know that it is still fresh and active. If there is no activity, please dispose of that yeast and use a different yeast for your challah dough.

OIL

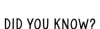

Oil adds smoothness and richness to the dough. Challah is a special bread, so we always use some oil (or other fat, like butter) to make it extra soft and flavorful.

Have you noticed that when you pour oil into a jar of dressing, the oil always rises up to the top? You have to shake that jar very hard to get the oil to mix with the other ingredients. And even then, as soon as you walk away, there goes the oil—back to the top of the jar again!

The Jewish people are compared to oil. Wherever we go in the world, we hold onto our special mitzvot that keep us distinct and separate. We always add lots of flavor and richness to every place we live in, but only when we stay like "oil," true to ourselves, do we maintain that which makes us unique.

Sometimes we may think that we want to be like everyone else, but it's those things that make us stand apart that make us special and add a flavor to the world that only we can bring!

So, celebrate your uniqueness, as a one-of-a-kind human being! By being *you*, you will make the world a much better place.

EGGS

Even though that oil keeps wanting to separate, we really want it to blend in nicely to make this dough delicious and soft.

Eggs can do it! They are up to the task!

Eggs are the "binders." They bring everything together and also add lots of flavor and richness to the challah.

We can be "connectors" too!

There is so much that we all share. When we remember that, it's easy to bring everyone together. When all the ingredients blend, it creates the magic that is challah.

DID YOU KNOW?

BLOOD IS NOT KOSHER! IF AN EGG HAS EVEN ONE DROP OF BLOOD, WE DON'T WANT IT IN OUR CHALLAH. BE SURE TO CHECK EACH EGG FOR BLOOD SPOTS BEFORE YOU DROP IT IN THE CHALLAH DOUGH. IF THE EGG HAS BLOOD, DISCARD IT AND USE A DIFFERENT EGG.

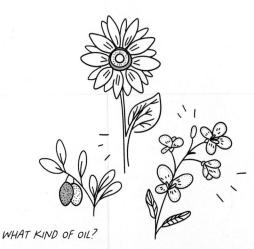

WHAT KIND OF OIL?

Most of my sweet challah recipes call for a flavorless oil, like canola oil. Grapeseed oil, vegetable oil, or sunflower oil are all good replacement choices for canola oil. Butter (or a pareve substitute, like Earth Balance or margarine) makes for a very decadent challah, and we have recipes with that in this book too. When the recipe is for a savory challah, it will often call for extra virgin olive oil.

SALT

Whoa!
Slow down there! The yeast can't seem to stop gobbling up the sugar!

Even though the challah will puff up real big—and quickly, too—if the yeast is allowed to go to town on that dough, it will eventually puff up way too much and just collapse!

Salt is like the adult in the room. It controls the chaos so the yeast can have fun, but not too much fun—otherwise, in the end, nobody will be happy.

Salt plays a super important role in the challah recipe. However, since it likes to stop the yeast from growing, it has to be put in at the right time. Only put in the salt after the yeast has already been activated in the sugar and water. Then the salt can join the party and still control things without ruining the rising fun!

WHAT KIND OF SALT?

My favorite salt to use in a challah dough is fine sea salt. It isn't bitter like table salt, and the small crystals help it blend easily into the dough.

A FEW THINGS THE SALT DOES:

~ Salt slows down the rising, allowing the yeast to ferment in the dough more slowly and give much more flavor to the challah.

~ Salt tightens the dough, holding it together, so the dough isn't all floppy and we can make beautiful braids and shapes with it.

~ Salt prevents the yeast from gobbling up all the sugar. The remaining sugar can then help form a beautiful golden crust, instead of leaving the challah pale and sad.

~ Salt is also a preservative. This means it will keep the challah fresh for longer.

CAN YOU GUESS WHAT THE SALT IS IN OUR LIVES?

Yup. It's the rules.

And even though sometimes we wish they weren't there and we could just go crazy, we know that everything works out better in the end when there are boundaries and order.

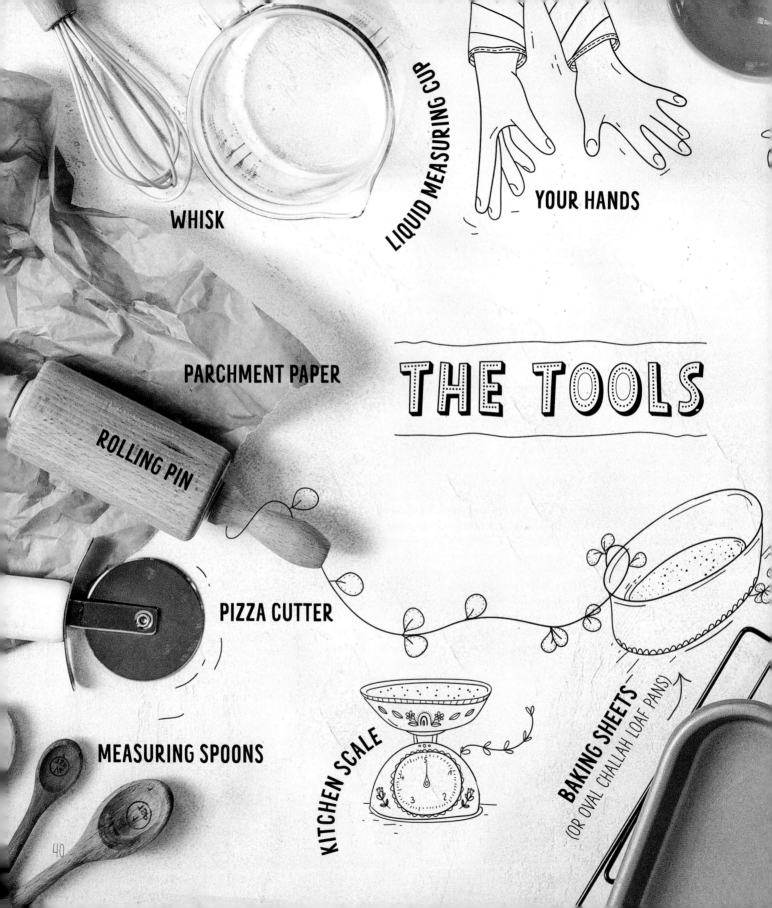

WHISK

LIQUID MEASURING CUP

YOUR HANDS

PARCHMENT PAPER

THE TOOLS

ROLLING PIN

PIZZA CUTTER

MEASURING SPOONS

KITCHEN SCALE

BAKING SHEETS
(OR OVAL CHALLAH LOAF PANS)

DRY MEASURING CUPS

THE BIG BOWL
(or an electric mixer)

MIXING SPOON
(if not using a mixer)

PASTRY BRUSH

YOU DON'T NEED MANY SUPPLIES TO MAKE A CHALLAH!

To make the dough all you really need is a big bowl and your hands.

That said, having the right tools on hand always makes baking more fun and more successful.

Pictured on this page are some basic tools that can help make the challah-making experience smoother for you. Since these tools are what I call "the basic ones," I'm going to assume you have them already, and I won't list them in the equipment list before each recipe.

Some recipes in this book call for more specialized tools or supplies. I'll list them in the equipment list on that page so you can make sure you have them available before you start making the recipe.

SILICONE BAKING MAT

COOLING RACK

BENCH SCRAPER

41

HELPFUL BAKING TERMS

MISE EN PLACE:

When chefs make a recipe, they prepare everything before they start cooking.

All the ingredients are chopped and measured and prepared in bowls, ready to add in when needed.

Having all your ingredients prepared and ready is called "*mise en place*," a French term that means "everything in its place."

It's a great way to cook and bake because it can make the whole process easier and so much more fun. It's also a great way to live, even outside of the kitchen!

Need to have your backpack packed up, lunch prepared, and test signed before school starts in the morning? Try applying "*mise en place*" to that too, and see how much smoother and less stressful your mornings become!

We can also remember that Hashem, the Chef of Life, who is cooking up everything in this world, has the ultimate "*mise en place*." All the pieces of creation are in place. When we simply focus on working with the ingredients He has prepared for us, the recipe for life becomes a lot easier to get right!

HOW DO YOU PRONOUNCE THAT?

MISE EN PLACE IS A FRENCH TERM AND IT IS PRONOUNCED, "MEEZ-ON-PLAHS" (IF YOU SAY IT WITH A SNOOTY FRENCH ACCENT YOU'LL SOUND VERY FANCY).

BUTTER: COLD / SOFTENED / MELTED

Often in a recipe, it will specify at what temperature the butter or margarine should be. This is important, as it will change the way the butter works in that recipe.

Cold butter: If the recipe says to use cold butter, keep it in the fridge until you're ready to use it.

Softened butter: Take the butter out of the fridge when you're gathering up all your ingredients. Then it will be warmed up and easier to incorporate into the rest of the recipe.

Melted butter: Melt the butter in a pot on the stove or in the microwave before putting it into the recipe.

BLOOM OR "PROOF" THE YEAST

Blooming (also known as "proofing") is the way we test yeast to see if it is active (especially if the yeast has been in our cupboard for a while). The yeast is put into very warm water, about 100-110° F, and allowed to sit for a while. If the yeast is still alive, it will start bubbling or foaming.

CARAMELIZE

To caramelize means to slowly sauté, cook, or roast foods that have natural sugars in them. Doing so causes the sugars to come out and start turning into caramel, giving the food a beautiful brown color and a richer, more delicious flavor.

CHOP / DICE / CHIFFONADE

CHOP means to cut into chunks.

DICE means to cut into little cubes or squares.

CHIFFONADE is a method of cutting greens like lettuce or basil. The leaf is rolled up tightly, and then cut into strips. This makes the cut greens look like ribbons.

CURDLE

When milk goes sour, little pieces rise to the top. This is called curdling. Gross, throw it out! Sometimes, however, a recipe calls for buttermilk, which is basically milk that has been fermented, which means soured in a way that makes it safe and healthy. We can make our own buttermilk by adding acid like vinegar or lemon juice to fresh milk, which will make it curdle right away. When we use this in a recipe, it adds tanginess to the final taste.

DUST

To dust means to lightly sprinkle a powder, like confectioners sugar or flour, over the finished baked goods. Using a sifter or special dusting tool will help you get a nice even powdering.

GARNISH

This means to decorate the final food before we serve it. This is usually done with an ingredient that is in the food, or that will add some color and flavor to the final dish.

GREASE THE PAN

This is how we make sure that whatever we are baking will come out of the baking dish or pan easily, without sticking to it. Grease the pan by rubbing or lightly smearing some butter or margarine all over its inside surface, or by spraying it with a cooking oil spray or baking spray.

PREHEAT THE OVEN

Before putting our challah in the oven to bake, it is important to make sure the oven has already reached the temperature specified in that challah's recipe. We preheat the oven by turning it on in advance, giving it the time it needs to heat up. Most ovens have a light or indicator that will tell you when the oven has reached the desired temperature.

SET

This means that the food is no longer "jiggly" and is now fully solid (such as in, "the eggs need to be set," or, "the filling will set while it's cooling").

WHISK

Whisking is a way of getting air into what we are mixing. We do this by using a whisk (or a fork) and mixing in a vertical circular up-and-down motion instead of 'round and 'round.

DOUGHS & DON'TS!
HELPFUL TIPS ABOUT CHALLAH DOUGH

DON'T

DON'T ADD TOO MUCH FLOUR.

If the dough feels very sticky and you have already put in all the flour the recipe called for, don't add more flour. Just put a little oil on your hands before kneading it as well as you can and let it rise for 30-45 minutes. Then try working with it again. While you're braiding, you can sprinkle on more flour to help along the braiding if the strands are still too sticky to work with. Better yet, spray some oil spray on the strands—they won't dry out but also won't stick to everything!

DON'T REDO YOUR BRAIDS.

If you don't like the way your braiding turned out, don't keep taking the strands apart and working with them again. Rolling out the dough many times will toughen it up and ruin the softness of your challah.

Better lopsided and soft than pretty and tough … right? And remember, each time you braid a challah, you get better at it. *Practice makes perfect.*

DON'T LET THE DOUGH RISE FOR TOO LONG!

The dough should rise until it has about doubled in size. In a very warm spot this can take about 1.5-2.5 hours. If your kitchen is cooler, it may take a bit longer. If the dough has doubled in size and you don't have time to braid it yet, punch it down to let out some of the air, and let it rise again until doubled in size.

If you know you won't be able to braid and bake for a long time, you can leave the dough to rise in the fridge for up to 24 hours.

DO!

USE ROOM TEMPERATURE INGREDIENTS.

• Eggs should be removed from the fridge a few hours before making the dough, or placed (unopened) in lukewarm water to warm up.

• When using melted butter, it should be warm—not hot.

• Dry yeast can be used straight from the fridge or freezer; it doesn't have to be warmed up. Fresh yeast should come to room temperature. If freezing fresh yeast, give it 30-60 minutes to come to room temperature before using it in your challah dough.

LEAVE THE DOUGH ALONE FOR A BIT.

After you mix in all the ingredients, you can just leave your dough alone for a little while (20-30 minutes is good). This step, called the "autolyse," gives the dough time to start developing on its own. By the time you start kneading it, the gluten will already have started to tighten and the kneading will be much quicker and easier.

LET YOUR DOUGH RELAX.

When you're ready to braid your challah, divide all the dough into the size pieces you want to work with, and let them rest for a few minutes before rolling them out. When the dough is rested, the gluten relaxes, which makes it much easier to roll and shape.

ROLL YOUR STRANDS OUT ON A COUNTERTOP OR TABLE.

Rolling the dough in midair will never be nearly as effective as rolling it on a hard surface. Plus, the results are always much prettier that way.

MAKE SURE TO HAVE FUN!

Turn on music, bake with people you love, and think about how amazing the challah will be and what a beautiful mitzvah this is. Challah always comes out better when you make it while in a good mood!

WE NEED TO KNEAD

Kneading is how we strengthen the gluten in the dough, making it elastic and resilient so it will be stretchy enough to braid and able to hold together in the heat of the oven. Kneading also gives the challah the smooth and tight "crumb" (inside of the bread) that makes challah so good.

Stand on a stool or put your dough on a surface that is lower than your counter. Push the dough away from you with the heel of your hand, stretching it out.

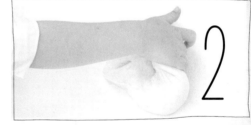

Now fold it back in towards you. Using a bench scraper to scrape the dough off the surface might make this easier.

Rotate the dough about ¼ turn, and repeat steps 1–3 until the dough feels like it holds together and is smooth and elastic. This usually happens after about 10 minutes of vigorous kneading. (Lightly sprinkle flour as needed throughout the kneading process.)

The dough is ready when:
1. It doesn't spill over your hands when you lift it up, but holds together fairly well.
2. It bounces back when you gently poke your finger into it.

RULES OF RISING

DO THE RISING READINESS TEST

How do you know when your dough is well-kneaded and ready to rise? Here are a few ways to check.

1. The poke test: Poke your finger into the dough. If the dough bounces back, you know it's good to go!

2. Lift up the dough and see if it all stays together in a ball or spills over your hands. If it holds together, that's good. If it's spilling over the sides, it needs more kneading time.

3. Stretch out a piece of the dough and see how quickly it tears. It should be elastic enough that you can stretch it out without it tearing right away.

RISE THE DOUGH IN A GLASS OR METAL BOWL

It holds the heat better than plastic. You can also run some hot water over the bowl to heat it up (and then dry it well before putting in the dough). This will help the dough rise faster.

PROTECT THE DOUGH

Put a bit of oil into the bowl before you place your dough inside. Roll the dough around in the oil so it's all coated (this will keep it from drying out while it's rising). Then, cover the bowl, either with plastic wrap (like Saran wrap) or with a damp dishtowel (wet a dishtowel with hot water, wring it well so it doesn't drip, and place it over the challah bowl).

STANDARD RISING

You don't want the dough to rise too quickly or it won't develop any flavor. On the other hand, while slow rises (see below) can give a really nice flavor to the challah, if you're leaving the dough on the counter or in the kitchen, you don't want it to rise too long either.

The best temperature for rising is about 75–85°F (24–29°C). Find a nice warm spot in the kitchen, and rise until the dough is about doubled in size. At this temperature it should take approximately 1.5–2 hours.

SLOW (COLD) RISING

The dough can also be put in the fridge to rise for up to 24 hours. It should be covered well with Saran wrap (or stored in a large bag, like an unscented garbage bag) and coated in a little oil, so it doesn't dry out when rising.

Make sure there is plenty of room—the dough will grow really big in the fridge, but it won't over-rise, so don't worry about that. When you take the dough out of the fridge, you can let out all the air and start braiding it right away. You don't have to let the dough warm up first.

QUICK RISING

Sometimes you just don't have the time and need that dough to rise extra quickly! The highest temperature you can let it rise at is 90°F (32°C). Higher than that and the dough might start baking.

Here's a method for getting the dough to rise extra quickly:

✾ While you're making the dough, place a pan of warm water at the bottom of your oven and preheat the oven to the lowest temperature. Turn off the oven.

✾ Cover the dough, place it in the oven, and close the oven door.

✾ The hot water at the bottom of the oven will make it nice and steamy, and the warmth and steam will make your dough rise quickly.

HOW TO MAKE A CHALLAH

A Basic Guide

Challah is easy! Challah is fun! Challah is delicious!

If you just throw all the ingredients together in a bowl and leave it alone, it will probably still be good!

But what's that you say?
You want to be a Challah Superstar?
Yeah, I hear you. That is totally possible.

If that's what you're going for, let's discuss a few things about making challah that will be very helpful on your journey to becoming a world-dominating challah baking master.

TEN STEPS TO BECOMING A CHALLAH SUPERSTAR

THE PREP STEP

1 Be sure that your ingredients are all available and at room temperature. If making a recipe with eggs, take the eggs out of the fridge and allow them to come to room temperature before starting. Make sure you have all the necessary equipment. Read through the recipe a few times and envision making it in your head. Okay, now you're ready!

HAPPY YEAST, HAPPY CHALLAH **2**

Create a nice environment for your yeast to get active in. Yeast thrives on warmth and sweetness, so be sure to use water that is nice and warm (see "The Ingredients" on page 36 for more specifics). Put something sweet in the water, like sugar or honey, to help kickstart the yeast growth, and then add in the yeast and give it a little stir to dissolve.

SAY NO TO DRY DOUGH **3**

Put in your liquids first and then add the flour. Once you put the flour in, you can't take it out, so always add in the flour gradually. The more often you make challah, the more comfortable you will be with the stickier doughs and you will know when to stop adding flour. Always leave out the last few cups and add them in a bit at a time. Stop when the dough is able to pull away from the bowl—remember you can always add in more flour as you're kneading.

THE NEED TO KNEAD

Kneading the dough is not just about mixing the ingredients together. It stretches out the gluten in the flour and builds a dough that is stretchy and bouncy and all the things we love about challah. So don't skimp on this step. Put on some music, get yourself some height (like a kitchen stool), and roll up your sleeves. There is work to do, and the reward will be sweet. For more kneading tips see "Doughs and Don'ts" on page 44.

4

RISE TO THE OCCASION **5**

This is the most important part of the challah making process. But it also requires major patience. There are ways to slow it down or speed it up (for details on all that see "Rules of Rising" on page 46), but no matter what, it's always a process. We need to wait and allow the dough to grow with time. This is when the magic happens. Let the dough rise until it at least doubles in size.

HOLY DOUGH=CHALLAH **6**

Once the dough has risen, we take off a small piece of the dough and recite a blessing (this depends on the size of the dough we're making; please see page 27 for instructions and the blessing text).

This is how regular dough becomes magical challah. You are well on your way to super-challah stardom.

Now's your chance to wow with endless possibilities of challah shapes. This is how we honor the Shabbat and beautify the mitzvah of challah. Try one of the dozens of challah shapes in this book or make up some new ones yourself! Here's where you get to play with your food and let your creativity shine.

7 BRAID OF HONOR

But we already let it rise! Yes, and now we let it rise again! Once the dough is braided, we need to let it fill up with more air so that it will be fluffy and wonderful. Place the braided dough on a parchment paper-lined baking sheet, or in challah loaf pans that have been sprayed or rubbed with oil.

Lightly cover your braided challahs with a dishcloth and wait until they're puffy and proud. In about 45 minutes (see "Rules of Rising" on page 46 for more specifics) they should be ready to shine! Paint them with an egg glaze to get that nice glow, and then sprinkle them with your favorite topping.

RISE AND SHINE! 8

BAKE UP THE BABIES 9

Now we bake the challah. Remember that the challahs will continue to rise in the oven, so make sure to give them plenty of room to grow. Most challahs bake at 350°F for about 30 minutes (for a medium-sized challah).

Some recipes call for different baking temperatures, so always make sure you're baking at the right temperature. Preheat the oven while your braided challahs are getting their final rising, and make sure the oven is at the desired temperature before putting the challahs in the oven. Try not to open the oven door until the challah is ready to come out of the oven. If your oven has a light, use that to peek in on your baking challah babies!

10 COOL DOWN

When your challahs come out of the oven they should be golden brown on top and browned on the bottom. When you tap the bottom they should feel crisp and sound hollow. This means that the challah is baked all the way through. Take the challahs off the baking sheet and place them onto a cooling rack so those crisp bottoms don't get soggy. Wait until they have totally cooled off before wrapping and storing.

YOU ARE NOW A CHALLAH SUPERSTAR.
I tremble before your challah awesomeness.

THE RECIPES

CHALLAH ALL DAY

THE RECIPES

51

USE THESE STEP-BY-STEP PHOTOS TO GUIDE YOU IN MAKING ALL OF THE DOUGHS IN THE CLASSIC CHALLAH SECTION.

1 Pour **warm water** into a bowl. Add the **sugar** and **yeast**. Stir to combine.

At this point, add whatever sweetener the recipe calls for (sometimes it may be honey instead of sugar).

2 Add the rest of the liquids, such as **eggs**, **oil**, and **vanilla extract** (and any other liquid the recipe calls for), and stir well to combine.

3 Add the **salt** and **flour**, adding only as much flour as needed for the dough to pull away from the sides of the bowl. Add the flour gradually—don't worry if you use less than the recipe calls for.

4 Knead **dough** until smooth and elastic. Add a bit of oil in the challah bowl and roll the dough around in it. Cover the bowl and let dough rise until doubled in size, or overnight in the fridge.

5 When the dough is puffy, punch it down to let out the air, and do the challah separation and blessing, if required.

See page 27 for detailed instructions.

6 Preheat the oven. Braid or shape dough, then allow to rise again. **Glaze with egg** or other glaze as directed, and top with your favorite **toppings**.

Follow baking instructions for each recipe.

READ THIS FIRST!

STUFF YOU NEED TO KNOW ABOUT THIS BOOK
BEFORE YOU START BAKING

EGG GLAZE: 1 egg yolk, beaten with 2 tsp water, unless otherwise specified; for an egg-free glaze, try honey or silan date syrup

FLOUR: unbleached, all-purpose flour, unless otherwise stated

YEAST: instant or quick-rise active dry yeast

SALT: fine sea salt

SUGAR: white refined, unless otherwise stated; honey can be substituted (3/4 cup honey to 1 cup sugar)

PAREVE:

All challahs in this book are pareve unless otherwise stated. Halachically, challahs that are dairy or meat must be shaped differently than regular challah or bread to identify them clearly as such, or made in a small enough quantity that can all be eaten in one meal.

BLESSING ON THE CHALLAHS: The blessing recited on bread is generally *hamotzi*. However, there are certain factors that could change the blessing to that of *mezonot*. Many of the recipes in this book may require the blessing of *mezonot* rather than *hamotzi*. Halachic opinions vary in this regard. It is therefore recommended that if in question as to the blessing, one should consult with their own halachic authority.

SYMBOLS TO KNOW

LEVELS

The recipes are marked with their level of difficulty. Those with one black star are the easiest. Three black stars indicate an advanced skill level.

Don't let that scare you off, though. A recipe is often marked with three stars because it has extra steps or requires adult supervision at certain points. Look through the recipe well to see if it seems like something you can accomplish. *And then, reach for the stars!*

CAUTION!

This warning sign is cute, but don't let it fool you.

Sometimes the recipes require working with hot oil or other dangerous things. Be sure to ask an adult if this is a recipe you can do yourself, or if perhaps they should step in for some parts of the recipe.

LITTLE MITTS

This symbol indicates that in this recipe there are things the very littlest hands can do.

When you see this symbol on the page, it means there is lots in this recipe little hands can help with. If you see this symbol near one particular step of the recipe, it refers specifically to that step.

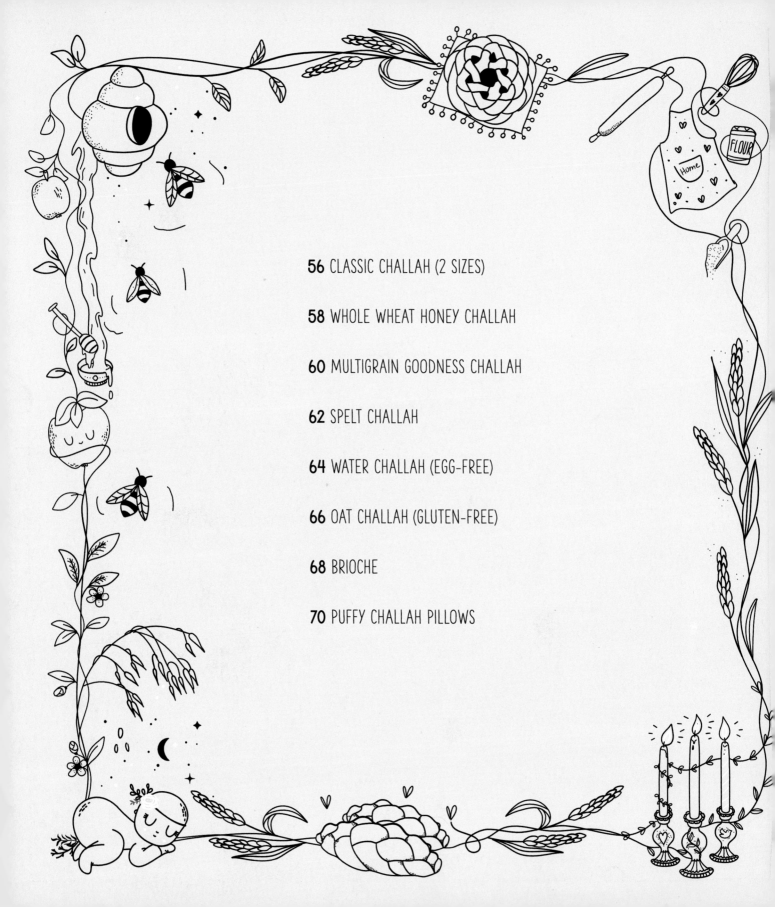

CLASSIC. NEVER BASIC.

CHALLAH CLASSICS

THE ROYAL 6-BRAID
page 268

CLASSIC CHALLAH

YIELD: 8 MEDIUM CHALLAHS (LARGE RECIPE) / 4 MEDIUM CHALLAHS (MEDIUM RECIPE)

I'm just going to say it. This is the most perfect challah recipe on Earth. This classic recipe is the base for almost every other recipe in this book! Once you master this recipe, you are on your way to challah stardom. I have offered it in two quantities. If you make the larger recipe, you will have enough to take off a piece of dough for the special challah blessing. See page 27 for all the details about this mitzvah.

Large Recipe:

- 4¾ cups warm water
- 1½ cups sugar
- 7 tsp yeast
- 1 cup oil
- 2 eggs, beaten
- 2 tsp vanilla extract
- 2½ Tbsp fine sea salt
- 13-15 cups all-purpose flour (approximately a 5 lb bag)

Medium Recipe:

- 2 cups water
- ¾ cup sugar
- 4½ tsp yeast
- 1 tsp vanilla extract
- 2 eggs, beaten
- ½ cup oil
- 1½ Tbsp fine sea salt
- 7-9 cups all-purpose flour

Glaze:

1 egg yolk, beaten with 2 tsp water

1. Pour the **warm** water into a bowl. Add the sugar and **yeast**; stir to combine.

2. Add the **oil**, **eggs**, and **vanilla**; stir well.

3. Add the **salt** and **13 cups flour**, adding the **remaining flour** as needed until the dough pulls away from the sides of the bowl.

4. Knead until smooth and elastic. Put a bit of oil in the challah bowl and roll the dough around in it. Cover the bowl, and let rise in a warm spot for 2-3 hours, or overnight in the fridge.

5. When the dough is puffy, punch it down to let out the air. Then do the challah separation. If making the large recipe, do it with the blessing. If making the medium recipe, do it without the blessing.*

6. Braid, then **glaze with egg**, and top with your favorite toppings.

7. Allow to rise for another 1-1½ hours, then bake in a 350°F oven for 30 minutes.

*SEE PAGE 27 FOR CHALLAH SEPARATION INSTRUCTIONS

THE MAGEN DAVID BRAID
page 272

WHOLE WHEAT HONEY CHALLAH

YIELD: 4 MEDIUM CHALLAHS

Whoever said healthy and delicious don't go together obviously never tasted my whole wheat challah! Once you try it I know you'll agree—nutritious rhymes with delicious for a reason!

3 cups warm water

¾ cup honey, plus more for drizzling

6 tsp yeast

½ cup oil

3 eggs, beaten

1 tsp vanilla extract

1½ Tbsp fine sea salt

8-9 cups whole wheat flour

Glaze:

1 egg yolk, beaten with 2 tsp water

Toppings:

Savory Oat Crunch (*page 232*)
or old-fashioned oats

1. Pour the **warm water** into a bowl. Add the **honey** and **yeast**; stir to combine.

2. Add the **oil**, **eggs**, and **vanilla**; stir well.

3. Add the **salt** and **8 cups flour**, adding the remaining flour as needed until the dough pulls away from the sides of the bowl.

4. Knead until smooth and elastic. Put a bit of oil in the challah bowl, and roll the dough around in it. Cover the bowl, and let rise in a warm spot for 3-4 hours, or overnight in the fridge.

5. When the dough is puffy, punch it down to let out the air, then do the challah separation without a blessing.*

6. Braid as desired, then **glaze with egg**. Drizzle on some **honey**, then sprinkle with **oat topping** for a nice crunchy finish.

7. Allow to rise for another 1-1½ hours, then bake in a 350°F oven for 35 minutes.

*SEE PAGE 27 FOR CHALLAH SEPARATION INSTRUCTIONS

Whole wheat challah tends to be very dense, so be sure to give it lots of extra rising time for a fluffier challah!

12-STRAND BASKET WEAVE
page 270

Full of multi grains,
bursting with seeds,
nuts, and fruit...
I call this one the
ABUNDANCE CHALLAH!

MULTIGRAIN GOODNESS CHALLAH

YIELD: 4 MEDIUM CHALLAHS

This is not your typical challah! We're talking super hearty with five healthy grains, mountains of seeds, and just the right amount of crunch. This recipe is a celebration of the bounty of goodness that is Hashem's creation. This is a sticky dough and will not be as elastic as a classic challah dough. Don't worry — it will become less sticky as it rises; stickiness means it will not be dry!

3½ cups warm water

½ cup honey

4½ tsp yeast

1 large egg, beaten

¼ cup extra-virgin olive oil

2 cups rye flour

2 cups whole wheat flour

¼ cup ground golden flaxseed

¼ cup old-fashioned oats

½ cup roasted, unsalted pumpkin seeds

½ cup roasted, unsalted sunflower seeds

¼ cup chia seeds

¼ cup millet

½ cup craisins, optional

1½ Tbsp fine sea salt

4 cups bread flour or high-gluten flour

Glaze:

1 egg yolk, beaten with 2 tsp water

Toppings:

Sunflower seeds, pumpkin seeds, oats, and coarse sea salt

1. Pour the **warm water** into a bowl. Add the **honey** and **yeast**; stir to combine.

2. Add the **egg** and **oil**; stir well.

3. Add the **rye flour**, **whole wheat flour**, **flaxseed**, and **oats**; stir to combine. Add the **pumpkin seeds**, **sunflower seeds**, **chia seeds**, **millet**, and **craisins** (if desired); mix well to incorporate. Add the **salt** and **bread flour**.

4. Knead until dough comes together. Put a bit of oil in the challah bowl and roll the dough around in it. Cover the bowl, and let rise in a warm spot for 3-4 hours, or overnight in the fridge.

5. When the dough is puffy, punch it down to let out the air, then do the challah separation without a blessing.*

6. Braid as desired, then **glaze with egg**, and top with **seeds** of choice.

7. Allow to rise for another 1-1½ hours, then bake in a 350°F oven for 35 minutes.

*SEE PAGE 27 FOR CHALLAH SEPARATION INSTRUCTIONS

12-STRAND SIMCHA BRAID
page 266

SPELT CHALLAH

YIELD: 4 MEDIUM CHALLAHS

Spelt is an ancient grain that we read about in the Torah. It is one of the five bread grains that we can make challah from. Therefore, we can say the blessing of Hamotzi on it. Since spelt has less gluten than wheat, and is a less cultivated grain than wheat, many people find it easier to digest. But don't think that this makes it any less yummy! This spelt challah tastes like any regular challah (maybe better!), and this is the challah that I make each week in my home for Shabbat. It's always fun to tell the guests that it's spelt and see the surprised look on their faces!

1½ cups warm water

¾ cup sugar

4½ tsp yeast

½ cup oil

3 eggs

½ tsp vanilla extract

1½ Tbsp fine sea salt

8-9 cups white spelt flour

Glaze:

1 egg yolk, beaten with 2 tsp water

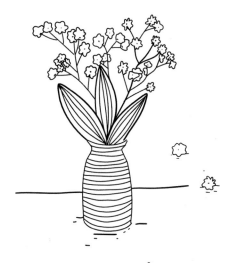

1. Pour the **warm water** into a bowl. Add the **sugar** and the **yeast**; stir to combine.

2. Add the **oil**, **eggs**, and **vanilla extract**; stir well.

3. Add the **salt** and **7 cups flour**, adding the remaining flour as needed until the dough pulls away from the sides of the bowl.

4. Knead until smooth and elastic. Put a bit of oil in the challah bowl, and roll the dough around in it. Cover the bowl, and let rise in a warm spot for 1½-2 hours or overnight in the fridge.

5. When the dough is puffy, punch it down to let out the air, then do the challah separation without a blessing.*

6. Braid as desired, and **glaze with egg**.

7. Allow to rise for another 1-1½ hours, then bake in a 350°F oven for 35 minutes.

*SEE PAGE 27 FOR CHALLAH SEPARATION INSTRUCTIONS

6-STRAND CLASSIC BRAID
page 266

WATER CHALLAH (EGG-FREE)

YIELD: 4 MEDIUM CHALLAHS

This challah is great for those who don't eat eggs. But even if you do eat eggs, you will still love this water challah. It has a beautiful texture and more breadlike flavor than other challah. My family gets very excited when I make this challah for Shabbat, and yours will too once you cut into the crusty loaf!

3 cups warm water

¾ cup sugar

4 ½ tsp yeast

2 Tbsp oil

1½ Tbsp fine sea salt

8-9 cups all-purpose or spelt flour

Topping Options:

Honey

Silan (date syrup)

Olive oil

Flour

1. Pour **warm water** into a bowl. Add the **sugar** and **yeast**; stir to combine.

2. Add the **oil** and stir.

3. Add the **salt** and **7 cups flour**, adding the **remaining flour** as needed until the dough pulls away from the sides of the bowl.

4. Knead until smooth and elastic. Put a bit of oil in the challah bowl, and roll the dough around in it. Cover the bowl, and let rise in a warm spot for 1½ -2 hours or overnight in the fridge.

5. When the dough is puffy, punch it down to let out the air, then do the challah separation without a blessing.*

6. Braid as desired, then glaze with **honey**, **silan**, or **olive oil**. Alternatively, dust with **flour** (*as pictured*).

7. Allow to rise for 1-1½ hours, then bake in a 375°F oven for 30 minutes.

*SEE PAGE 27 FOR CHALLAH SEPARATION INSTRUCTIONS

THIS CHALLAH RECIPE CAN REPLACE ANY OF THE RECIPES IN THE BOOK THAT CALL FOR THE CLASSIC CHALLAH DOUGH. IT ALSO WORKS BEST FOR ANY OF THE MORE PIZZA-DOUGH STYLE RECIPES IN THE BOOK, SUCH AS THE FOCACCIA, THE CHALLZONE, THE CHEESE-STUFFED CHALLAH AND THE DESSERT PIZZA!

CHALLAH SHAPE CREATED USING
SILICONE CHALLAH MOLD

★☆☆

OAT CHALLAH (GLUTEN-FREE)

YIELD: 4 MEDIUM CHALLAHS

For all those who can't eat gluten and feel deprived of the deliciousness of challah, this recipe is for you. Since this challah is made with a majority of oat flour, the only one of the five bread grains in the Torah that is gluten-free, it is considered real challah, which means that the blessing of *hamotzi* can be made on it. And as an extra bonus, if making a large enough quantity, the challah separation can be done with a blessing. *And did I mention that it's delicious?*

Equipment:

Handheld or stand mixer

Silicone challah pan, loaf pan, or muffin tins

Ingredients:

2 cups warm water

1 Tbsp sugar

6 tsp yeast

1 cup non-dairy milk

¾ cup oil

¾ cup honey

3 eggs

½ tsp vanilla extract

3 tsp fine sea salt

4 cups gluten-free oat flour

2 cups gluten-free all-purpose flour blend

1 Tbsp xanthan gum

Glaze:

1 egg yolk, beaten with 2 tsp water

Topping:

Gluten-free oats

honey

1. Pour the **warm water** into the bowl of a stand mixer fitted with the paddle attachment. (Alternatively, use a hand mixer.) Add the **sugar** and **yeast**; stir to combine.

2. Add the **milk**, **oil**, **honey**, **eggs**, and **vanilla extract**; stir well.

3. Add the **salt**, **flours**, and **xanthan gum**. Mix until incorporated, but don't overmix. The mixture will resemble a thick batter, not like a challah dough.

4. Cover the bowl, and let it rise in a warm spot for 1-1½ hours, until the batter is doubled in size.

5. Mix the batter again to let out the air, then do the challah separation without a blessing.*

6. Spoon the batter (about ¾ full) into greased pans. Allow to rise for another 30-45 minutes, then **glaze with egg**. Sprinkle challahs with **oats** and a drizzle of **honey**.

7. Bake in a 375°F oven for 35 minutes.

*SEE PAGE 27 FOR CHALLAH SEPARATION INSTRUCTIONS

ADD SOME EXTRA SWEETNESS AND TEXTURE TO THIS RICH CHALLAH WITH CRUNCHY SUGAR ON TOP!

ROLL UP BRIOCHE LOAF SHAPE
page 271

BRIOCHE

YIELD: 4 MEDIUM CHALLAHS OR 2 LARGE ROLLED BRIOCHE LOAVES (AS PICTURED)

The richest, stretchiest, most delicious and decadent challah ever. A traditional brioche uses a LOT of butter, so don't be scared off by the huge amounts of butter in this recipe. To make this challah pareve, use non-dairy milk and butter. Using water instead of milk will ensure that you can make the blessing of *hamotzi* on it to use for the challah at the Shabbat table.

Equipment:

Strong stand mixer,
such as a Magic Mill or Bosch.

Large loaf pan

Ingredients:

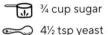

1 cup warm milk or water (see head note)

¾ cup sugar

4½ tsp yeast

6 eggs + 4 egg yolks

4 tsp vanilla extract

1½ Tbsp fine sea salt

8-9 cups all-purpose flour

16 oz (4 sticks) very cold butter

Glaze:

1 egg yolk, beaten with 2 tsp water

Topping:

Pearl sugar or Belgian waffle sugar

1. Pour the **warm milk** (or water) into the bowl of a stand mixer fitted with a paddle attachment. Add the **sugar** and **yeast**; stir to combine.

2. In another bowl, whisk the **eggs** and **yolks**, then add **vanilla**. Pour into the **yeast mixture**; stir to combine.

3. Add the **salt** and **flour**, adding the remaining flour as needed until the dough pulls away from the sides of the bowl. Mix at medium speed until the dough is smooth. If mixing by hand, oil your hands to make the job less messy; don't worry if the dough seems loose and sticky.

4. Add **butter**, half a stick at a time, mixing on low until each addition is well incorporated. It may take a while for the dough to come together — resist the urge to add more flour!

5. Once all the butter is incorporated, increase speed to high, and allow the dough to mix for 10-15 minutes; the dough should be smooth and pull away from the sides of the bowl.

6. Cover the bowl, and refrigerate for 8 hours or up to 24 hours. When you're ready to work with the dough, remove from the fridge and punch down to let out the air. Do the challah separation without a blessing.*

7. Braid as desired (*see page 271 for a traditional brioche shaping technique*), then glaze with **egg**, and sprinkle with **pearl sugar**. Allow to rise for another 45-60 minutes, then bake in a 350°F oven for 40-45 minutes.

*SEE PAGE 27 FOR CHALLAH SEPARATION INSTRUCTIONS

ROUND CHALLAH ROLL
page 257

★☆☆

PUFFY CHALLAH PILLOWS

YIELD: 2 9X13-INCH PANS OR 4 ROUND PULL-APART CHALLAHS

These gorgeous, soft, stretchy rolls are super easy to make — just throw all the ingredients into a bowl and knead. The only extra step is cooking a potato and mashing it (it's totally worth it). These buns last for days when kept in an airtight container and they freeze amazingly well too, so make them today and enjoy them for months. They will also still be super soft all through Shabbat, so for all the kids who like a good challah sandwich on Shabbat afternoon, this is your recipe! If you want to make the Hamotzi bracha on these, use water instead of the non-dairy milk.

Equipment:

2 9x13-inch pans or 4 8-inch round pans

Potato masher or ricer

Ingredients:

¾ cup warm non-dairy milk (or water)

¼ cup sugar

2½ tsp yeast

4½ cups all-purpose flour

1 cup plain mashed potatoes*

½ cup (1 stick) softened margarine or butter

2 large eggs

2 tsp fine sea salt

Glaze:

1 egg yolk, beaten with 2 tsp water

1. Pour **warm milk** (or water) into a large bowl. Add the **sugar** and **yeast**; stir to combine.

2. Add the **flour**, **mashed potatoes**, **margarine**, **eggs**, and **salt**; knead until smooth and elastic.

3. Put a bit of oil in the challah bowl, and roll the dough around in it. Cover the bowl, and let rise in a warm spot for 1½-2 hours or overnight in the fridge.

4. When the dough is puffy, punch it down to let out the air.*

5. Shape into balls. Place into 2 (9x13-inch) pans for individual rolls or into 4 (8-inch) round pans for pull-apart challahs. **Glaze with egg** (without a glaze these buns will also be fine and will resemble sandwich buns).

6. Allow to rise another 1-1½ hours, then bake in a 350°F oven for 20-25 minutes.

*NO CHALLAH SEPARATION REQUIRED, SEE PAGE 27 FOR DETAILS

NOTE: These rolls stay fresh in an airtight container for several days. Make sure to let them cool off completely before storing.

*For 1 cup mashed potato, all you need is 1 large potato (I like Yukon Gold, but you can use whatever you have). Don't worry too much about how big the potato is, you can use as little as ¾ cup mashed potatoes and as much as 1½ cups, and the recipe will still turn out great. If you have leftover mashed potatoes in your fridge, you can totally use that, but if it's salty, use less salt in the dough.

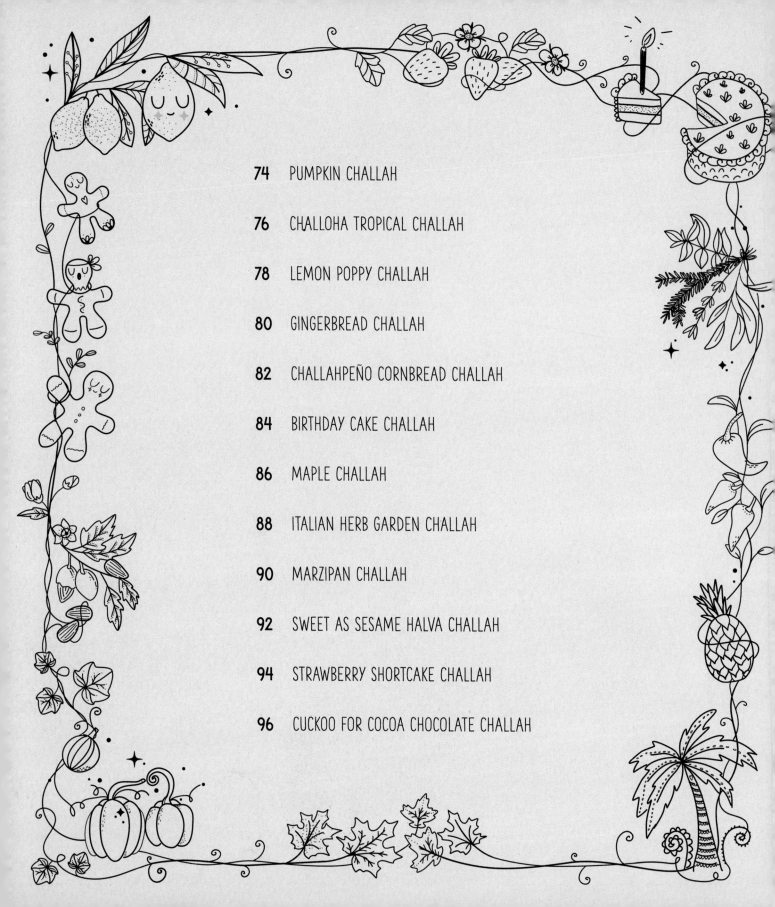

CHALLAH WITH PERSONALITY TO SPARE!

FULL OF FLAVOR

This recipe was featured in my first cookbook, but I offer it to you here with more options (like chocolate chips or maple pecan crunch), as well as brand new shapes, like the awesome pumpkin-shaped challah in this picture. In the past few years, ever since introducing pumpkin challah to the world, I have noticed more and more pumpkin challahs popping up on Thanksgiving tables, and that is just the way it should be. Challah, just like Thanksgiving, is all about remembering our blessings and their Source. Add some pumpkin to the mix, and you have all the good things in one delicious challah package.

PUMPKIN CHALLAH SHAPE
page 274

TO MAKE THE BEAUTIFUL FLORAL CUT-OUTS
FEATURED ON THIS CHALLAH,
SEE THE INSTRUCTIONS ON PAGE 255.

PUMPKIN CHALLAH

YIELD: 4 MEDIUM CHALLAHS OR PUMPKIN SHAPES, OR 20-24 MINI PUMPKIN CHALLAHS

Equipment:

Kitchen twine and scissors

Ingredients:

- 1½ cups warm water
- ¾ cup sugar
- 4½ tsp yeast
- 1 (15 oz) can of pumpkin purée (not pumpkin pie filling)
- ⅓ cup oil
- 2 eggs
- 1 tsp vanilla extract
- 1 tsp cinnamon
- 1½ tsp pumpkin pie spice
- Dash nutmeg
- Dash ground cloves
- 1½ Tbsp fine sea salt
- 7-8 cups all-purpose flour
- 1 cup mini chocolate chips, optional

Glaze:

1 egg yolk, beaten with 2 tsp water

Topping:

Savory option: Salted pepitas
Sweet option: Maple Pecan Oat Crunch
(*page 230*)

1. Pour the **warm water** into a bowl. Add the **sugar** and **yeast**; stir to combine.

2. Add the **pumpkin**, **oil**, **eggs**, **vanilla**, and **spices**; stir well.

3. Add the **salt** and **7 cups flour**; mix lightly. Add the **mini chocolate chips** (if desired), then mix, adding the remaining flour only as needed until the dough pulls away from the sides of the bowl.

4. Knead until smooth and elastic. Put a bit of oil in the challah bowl, and roll the dough around in it. Cover the bowl, and let rise in a warm spot for 1½-2 hours or overnight in the fridge.

5. When the dough is puffy, punch it down to let out the air, then do the challah separation without a blessing.*

6. Braid as desired, **glaze with egg**, and top with **toppings** of choice.

7. Allow to rise for another 45-60 minutes, then bake in a 350°F oven for 30 minutes.

*SEE PAGE 27 FOR CHALLAH SEPARATION INSTRUCTIONS

BRING THE TROPICS TO THE SHABBAT TABLE. THIS CHALLAH IS SWEET AND TANGY–WITH HINTS OF COCONUT–AND IS THE PERFECT WAY TO CELEBRATE A SUMMER SHABBAT!

PULL APART FLOWER CHALLAH
page 276

CHALLOHA TROPICAL CHALLAH

❦

YIELD: 16-18 ROLLS OR 4 CHALLAHS

Pineapple, coconut, and honey are having a party, and they want you to join! This is pure summer deliciousness. If you can find coconut chips, I highly recommend using as a topping — it adds an extra level of sweetness and crunch that takes this fabulous challah to new heights!

- 1 cup pineapple juice
- 1 cup low fat coconut milk
- ¾ cup honey
- 4½ tsp yeast
- ⅓ cup oil
- 1 egg
- 1 Tbsp vanilla extract
- ½ cup unsweetened ground coconut
- 1½ Tbsp fine sea salt
- 5½-6 cups high-gluten flour, divided

Glaze:

1 egg yolk, beaten with 2 tsp water

Topping:

Unsweetened coconut flakes

1. Mix the **pineapple juice** and **coconut milk** in a large glass measuring cup or bowl and microwave for 1 minute, until nice and warm (but not hot). Pour into the large mixing bowl.

2. Add the **honey** and **yeast** to the warm juice and milk in a large mixing bowl or the bowl of a stand mixer fitted with a dough hook attachment. Allow the yeast to bloom for about 10 minutes.

3. Add **oil**, **egg**, **vanilla**, and **ground coconut**. Mix well to combine.

4. Add **5 cups of flour** and **salt**, adding the remaining flour as needed until the dough pulls away from the sides of the bowl.

5. Knead dough until it comes together. Put a bit of oil in the challah bowl, and roll the dough around in it. Cover the bowl, and let it rise until doubled in size, at least 2½ hours or overnight in the fridge.

6. When the dough is puffy, punch it down to let out the air.*

7. Braid as desired, **glaze with egg**, and sprinkle with **coconut flakes**. Allow to rise another hour, then bake in a 350°F oven for 30 minutes.

*NO CHALLAH SEPARATION REQUIRED, SEE PAGE 27 FOR DETAILS
PLEASE NOTE: SINCE THIS CHALLAH IS MADE WITH JUICE AND MILK INSTEAD OF WATER, MANY OPINIONS WILL CONSIDER IT TO HAVE THE BLESSING OF MEZONOT. PLEASE CONSULT YOUR OWN HALACHIC AUTHORITY TO DETERMINE.

RECIPE NOTES:
✦ To prevent the dough from getting very heavy, make sure you avoid adding too much flour. It will be a pretty sticky dough — that's the way it should be.
✦ Because there's a lot of fat in this challah, it needs extra time to rise fully.

TWISTED TURBAN
page 258

LEMON POPPY CHALLAH

YIELD: 4 X 1 LB CHALLAHS OR 2 LARGE CHALLAHS

I'm not a huge poppy seed fan in general. However, there's one exception to that rule —
a lemon poppy muffin! The brightness of the lemon and the crunchiness of the poppy is just sublime.
So, I decided to create the challah version of my favorite muffin. Feel free to top it *before* baking with
Lemon Shortbread Streusel (*page 230*) and Lemon Glaze (*page 229*) *after* baking, for an extra sweet
and lemony finishing touch.

Equipment:

Zester or grater

Ingredients:

2 cups very warm water

¾ cup sugar

4½ tsp yeast

½ cup canola oil

¼ cup poppy seeds

2 large eggs, beaten

Zest of 2 lemons

2 tsp vanilla extract

½ tsp lemon extract

1½ Tbsp fine sea salt

8 cups all-purpose flour

Glaze:

1 egg yolk, beaten with 2 tsp water

Toppings:

Lemon Shortbread Streusel (*page 230*),
optional

Poppy seeds

Lemon Glaze (*page 229*), *optional*

PREP: Zest 2 lemons and set aside (see recipe note).

1. Pour the **warm water** into a bowl. Add the **sugar** and **yeast**; stir to combine.

2. Add the **oil, poppy seeds, eggs, lemon zest, vanilla extract**, and **lemon extract**; stir well.

3. Add the **salt** and **flour**, adding in only as much flour as needed for the dough to pull away from the sides of the bowl.

4. Knead until smooth and elastic. Put a bit of oil in the challah bowl, and roll the dough around in it. Cover the bowl, and let it rise in a warm spot for 1½ -2 hours or overnight in the fridge.

5. When the dough is puffy, punch it down to let out the air, then do the challah separation without a blessing.*

6. Braid as desired, **glaze with egg**, and sprinkle with **streusel** (if desired) or **poppy seeds**.

7. Allow to rise for another 45-60 minutes, then bake in a 350°F oven for 30 minutes.

8. Once challah is cool, drizzle with **glaze** (if desired).

*SEE PAGE 27 FOR CHALLAH SEPARATION INSTRUCTIONS

RECIPE NOTES:
Zesting means to grate the lemon peel on the smallest holes of a handheld fine grater. Only grate the yellow peel, not the white layer under it, which can be bitter!

4-STRAND CLASSIC BRAID
page 262

GINGERBREAD CHALLAH

YIELD: 4 X 1 LB CHALLAHS OR 2 LARGE CHALLAHS

This challah makes a gorgeous gift! With the addition of the crunchy speculoos (pronounced "speck-you-lows") cookies, which you may know as "Lotus" biscuits, it is an irresistibly delicious challah interpretation of the classic gingerbread cookie. If you want to make it really decadent, go ahead and drizzle some glaze on top as well, after the challah is baked and cooled.

2 cups warm water

½ cup molasses

½ cup dark brown sugar

4½ tsp yeast

½ cup oil

2 eggs

2 tsp ground ginger

1½ Tbsp fine sea salt

8-9 cups all-purpose flour

Glaze:

1 egg yolk, beaten with 2 tsp water

Topping:

Lotus Crumble (*page 230*)

Vanilla Glaze (*page 229*)

1. Pour the **warm water** into a bowl. Add the **molasses, brown sugar**, and **yeast**; stir to combine.

2. Add the **oil, eggs**, and **ground ginger**; stir well.

3. Add the **salt** and **8 cups flour**, adding the remaining flour as needed until the dough pulls away from the sides of the bowl.

4. Knead until smooth and elastic. Put a bit of oil in the challah bowl, and roll the dough around in it. Cover the bowl, and let it rise for 1½-2 hours, or overnight in the fridge.

5. When the dough is puffy, punch it down to let out the air, then do the challah separation without a blessing.*

6. Braid as desired, then **glaze with egg**. Sprinkle the **crumble** on top (if desired).

7. Allow to rise for another 45-60 minutes, then bake in a 350°F oven for 30 minutes. Allow to cool completely before drizzling on the **glaze** (if desired).

*SEE PAGE 27 FOR CHALLAH SEPARATION INSTRUCTIONS

THE 2-STRAND 4-STRAND
page 260

SERVE WITH:

Honey Sriracha or Chili Lime
Compound Butter (*page 238*)

CHALLAPEÑO CORNBREAD CHALLAH

YIELD: 4 X 1 LB CHALLAHS OR 8 MINI CHALLAHS (PICTURED)

All puns aside, cornbread challah can change your life.
Making a Mexican-themed Shabbat dinner perhaps?
This cornbread challah would work perfectly with a chili-style cholent.
More crumbly than a standard challah, but still more moist than a classic
cornbread, this challah works great to mop up all those spicy dips. Salsa, anyone?

1 cup non-dairy milk
(soy milk or almond milk)

1 Tbsp vinegar

½ cup very warm water

¾ cup sugar

4½ tsp yeast

2 eggs

½ cup oil

1 small chili pepper, finely diced

1 large jalapeño, finely diced

½ large red bell pepper, finely diced

1 bunch chives, finely diced

1½ Tbsp fine sea salt

3 cups cornmeal,
plus more for topping

4-5 cups bread flour

Glaze:

1 egg yolk, beaten with 2 tsp water

1. Make a **non-dairy buttermilk** by mixing the **non-dairy milk** and **vinegar**. Set it aside for a few minutes; it will begin to curdle, which is what makes it buttermilk.

2. Pour the **warm water** into a bowl. Add the **sugar** and **yeast**; stir to combine.

3. Add the **buttermilk mixture**, **eggs**, **oil**, and the **diced vegetables**; stir well.

4. Add the **salt**, **cornmeal**, and **4 cups flour**, adding the **remaining flour** as needed until the dough pulls away from the sides of the bowl.

5. Knead until smooth and elastic. Put a bit of oil in the challah bowl, and roll the dough around in it. Cover the bowl, and let rise for 1½-2 hours, or overnight in the fridge.

6. When the dough is puffy, punch it down to let out the air.*

7. Braid, **glaze with egg**, and sprinkle some **cornmeal** on top. You can also decorate the top with **minced chives**, if desired.

8. Allow to rise for another 30-45 minutes, then bake in a 350°F oven for 30 minutes.

*NO CHALLAH SEPARATION REQUIRED,
SEE PAGE 27 FOR DETAILS

BE SURE TO WEAR GLOVES WHEN HANDLING SPICY FOODS LIKE CHILI PEPPERS OR JALAPEÑOS, AND DON'T TOUCH YOUR FACE!

83

4-STRAND CLASSIC BRAID
page 266

BIRTHDAYS ARE A BIG DEAL!
EVEN IN THE TORAH WE SEE THAT
PEOPLE CELEBRATED THEIR
BIRTHDAYS. AVRAHAM THREW A
PARTY FOR HIS SON YITZCHAK'S
SECOND BIRTHDAY, AND KING
PHAROH THREW HIMSELF A MAJOR
BIRTHDAY PARTY!

BIRTHDAY CAKE CHALLAH

YIELD: 4 X 1LB CHALLAHS OR 1 LARGE BIRTHDAY NUMBER

This is the most celebratory challah ever! Does someone's birthday land on a Shabbat this year? Make them a birthday challah, and you can sing "happy birthday" at the beginning of the meal instead of waiting for dessert! *Jewish birthdays are a big deal*—the day you were born is the day that Hashem decided the world needs YOU! Your mazal shines extra strongly on this day, and you can use the day to grow spiritually, by giving extra tzedakah, making positive resolutions for the coming year, and learning more Torah on this day.

- 3 cups warm water
- ¾ cup sugar
- ¼ cup vanilla sugar
- 4½ tsp yeast
- ¼ cup oil
- 1 tsp butter flavoring (see notes)
- 1 tsp clear vanilla extract (see notes)
- 1½ Tbsp fine sea salt
- 8-9 cups unbleached all-purpose flour
- 1 cup colorful sprinkles

Glaze:

1 egg white, beaten with 1 tsp water

Topping:

Birthday Cake Crunch Topping (*page 230*)

RECIPE NOTES

♡ My goal was to get this challah to be as white as possible to make the sprinkles really pop. Vanilla extract usually gives challah a bit of a yellowish tinge, so I specify using a clear vanilla extract here. If you can't find it, don't worry, use the regular kind — the challah will just be a little less white.

♡ Find non-dairy butter flavoring at any baking supply store or online.

1. Pour the **warm water** into a bowl. Add the **sugar**, **vanilla sugar**, and **yeast**; stir to combine.

2. Add the **oil**, **butter flavoring**, and **vanilla extract**; stir well.

3. Add the **salt** and **8 cups flour**, adding the remaining flour as needed until the dough pulls away from the sides of the bowl.

4. Add the **sprinkles** towards the end of kneading once the dough has come together and is no longer wet and sticky, otherwise the colors will run.

5. Knead until smooth and elastic. Put a bit of oil in the challah bowl, and roll the dough around in it. Cover the bowl, and let it rise for 1½-2 hours, or overnight in the fridge.

6. When the dough is puffy, punch down to let out the air, and do the challah separation without a blessing.*

7. Braid as desired, **glaze with egg**, and top with **birthday cake topping**.

8. Allow to rise for another 45-60 minutes, then bake in a 350°F oven for 30 minutes.

*SEE PAGE 27 FOR CHALLAH SEPARATION INSTRUCTIONS

3-STRAND CLASSIC BRAID
page 260

MAPLE CHALLAH

YIELD: 4 X 1LB CHALLAHS OR 2 LARGE CHALLAHS

This challah is an ode to the country of my birth! Yup, I'm Canadian, and we are all about the maple tree and maple flavor on everything! I happen to love the flavor of maple syrup, and I use it often to sweeten foods as a healthier alternative to sugar.
This challah uses the addition of maple extract to add extra maple-y flavor. If your local store doesn't have it, try a specialty baking store, or an online store like Amazon.

1½ cups warm water

2 Tbsp sugar

4½ tsp yeast

½ cup maple syrup

⅓ cup canola oil

2 large eggs

1 tsp maple extract

1½ Tbsp fine sea salt

6½-7½ cups all-purpose flour

Glaze:

1 egg yolk, beaten with 2 tsp water

Topping:

Maple Pecan Oat Crunch
(*page 230*)

1. Pour the **warm water** into a bowl. Add the **sugar** and **yeast**; stir to combine.

2. Add the **maple syrup**, **oil**, **eggs**, and **maple extract**; stir well.

3. Add the **salt** and **6½ cups flour**, adding the **remaining flour** as needed until the dough pulls away from the sides of the bowl.

4. Knead until smooth and elastic. Put a bit of oil in the challah bowl, and roll the dough around in it. Cover the bowl, and let it rise in a warm spot for 1½-2 hours or overnight in the fridge.

5. When the dough is puffy, punch it down to let out the air, then do the challah separation without a blessing.*

6. Braid as desired, **glaze with egg**, and sprinkle with **maple crunch** (if desired).

7. Allow to rise for another 45-60 minutes, then bake in a 350°F oven for 30 minutes.

*SEE PAGE 27 FOR CHALLAH SEPARATION INSTRUCTIONS

Ingredients:

- 2 Tbsp pine nuts
- 3 cups warm water
- ¾ cup sugar
- 4½ tsp yeast
- 2 Tbsp extra-virgin olive oil
- ½ cup chopped sun-dried tomatoes
- ½ cup fresh basil leaves, finely chopped
- 2 Tbsp minced fresh thyme
- 1 Tbsp minced fresh sage
- 1-2 cloves garlic, grated or finely minced
- 2 Tbsp fine sea salt
- 8½ cups all-purpose flour

Topping:

Olive oil

Coarse sea salt

Fresh herbs

6-STRAND WEAVE BRAID
page 267

88

★★☆ EGG-FREE

ITALIAN HERB GARDEN CHALLAH

YIELD: 4 X 1LB CHALLAHS OR 2 LARGE CHALLAHS

Full of herby goodness and studded with color, this rustic challah is a favorite of mine! Make sure to have a good knife and cutting board on hand, and prepare all the herbs and vegetables before starting on the dough. This is an egg-free dough and works great for any pizza or focaccia recipe!

1. Toast **pine nuts** on a baking sheet in a 350°F oven for about 5-7 minutes, until lightly golden and fragrant; set aside.

2. Pour the **warm water** into a bowl. Add the **sugar** and **yeast**; stir to combine.

3. Add the **olive oil**, **sun-dried tomatoes**, **herbs**, **garlic**, and **toasted pine nuts**; mix to combine.

4. Add the **salt** and **8 cups flour**, adding the **remaining flour** as needed until the dough pulls away from the sides of the bowl.

5. Knead until smooth and elastic. Put a bit of oil in the challah bowl, and roll the dough around in it. Cover the bowl, and let it rise for 1½-2 hours or overnight in the fridge.

6. When the dough is all puffy, punch it down to let out the air, and do the challah separation without a blessing.*

7. Braid as desired, brush with **olive oil**, and sprinkle with **coarse sea salt** and **fresh herbs**.

8. Allow to rise for another 1-1½ hours, then bake in a 400°F oven for 25-30 minutes.

*SEE PAGE 27 FOR CHALLAH SEPARATION INSTRUCTIONS

SERVE WITH HERB BUTTER! SEE PAGE 238 FOR RECIPE

6-STRAND BASKET WEAVE
page 267

MARZIPAN CHALLAH

YIELD: 4 X 1LB CHALLAHS OR 2 LARGE CHALLAHS

There are only a few recipes from my first cookbook that cross over into this one, and this is one of them. It has been updated with even more amazing almond flavor and better texture than ever!

For extra marzipan yumminess, double the marzipan recipe below, and use the second half to fill the challah strands. The end result will be ooey gooey deliciousness. *See page 259 for instructions on filling challah strands.*

MAKE YOUR OWN MARZIPAN

Equipment:
Food processor

Ingredients:
- 1½ cups almond flour or almond meal
- ½ cup confectioners' sugar
- 2 tsp almond extract
- 1 egg white

Instructions:
Add all ingredients to a food processor fitted with the S-blade; pulse until it forms a paste. Use immediately or store in an airtight container in the fridge for up to 1 month.

- 2 cups warm water
- ½ cup sugar
- 4½ tsp yeast
- 1 cup marzipan filling (recipe follows)
- ⅓ cup oil
- 2 eggs
- 2 tsp almond extract
- 1 tsp vanilla extract
- 1 ½ Tbsp fine sea salt
- 7-8 cups all-purpose flour

Glaze:
1 egg yolk, beaten with 2 tsp water

Topping:
Sliced almonds

Pearl sugar

1. Pour the **warm water** into a bowl. Add the **sugar** and **yeast**; stir to combine.

2. Add **marzipan**, **oil**, **eggs**, **almond extract**, and **vanilla extract**; stir.

3. Add the **salt** and **7 cups flour**, adding the remaining flour as needed until the dough pulls away from the sides of the bowl.

4. Knead until smooth and elastic. Put a bit of oil in the challah bowl, and roll the dough around in it. Cover the bowl, and let rise in a warm spot for 1½-2 hours or overnight in the fridge.

5. When the dough is puffy, punch it down to let out the air, then do the challah separation without a blessing.*

6. Braid as desired, then **glaze with egg**, and sprinkle with **sliced almonds** and **pearl sugar**.

7. Allow to rise for another 1-1½ hours, then bake in a 350°F oven for 30 minutes.

*SEE PAGE 27 FOR CHALLAH SEPARATION INSTRUCTIONS

9-STRAND TRIPLED BASIC
page 269

92

SWEET AS SESAME
HALVA CHALLAH

YIELD: 4 X 1LB CHALLAHS
OR 2 LARGE CHALLAHS

With the addition of tahini paste and a generous pile of sesame seeds, this sesame challah hits all the notes —
a little sweet, a little savory, and full of nutty sesame flavor. The extra ingredients can weigh it down a bit, so be
sure to give this dough a longer rise so that you get a nice fluffy challah.

2 cups warm water

¾ cup sugar

4½ tsp yeast

½ cup sesame seeds

½ cup vanilla halva, crumbled

¼ cup tahini paste

2 eggs

1 tsp vanilla

1½ Tbsp fine sea salt

6-7 cups all-purpose flour

Oil, for greasing

Glaze:
1 egg yolk, beaten with 2 tsp water

Topping:
Sesame seeds

Halva Pistachio Crumble
(recipe on page 230)

1. Pour the **warm water** into a bowl. Add the **sugar**
   and **yeast**; stir to combine.

2. Add the **sesame seeds**, **halva**, **tahini**, **eggs**, and
   vanilla; stir well.

3. Add the **salt** and **6 cups flour**, adding the
   remaining flour as needed until the dough pulls
   away from the sides of the bowl.

4. Knead until smooth and elastic. Put a bit of **oil**
   in the challah bowl and roll the dough around in
   it. Cover the bowl, and let rise for 2-3 hours, or
   overnight in the fridge.

5. When the dough is puffy, punch it down to let
   out the air.*

6. Braid, **glaze with egg** and sprinkle with **sesame
   seeds** or **Halva Pistachio Crumble**.

7. Allow to rise for another 1-1½ hours, then bake in
   a 350°F oven for 30 minutes.

*NO CHALLAH SEPARATION REQUIRED, SEE PAGE 27 FOR DETAILS

2 5-STRAND TOP TWISTS MAKE A HEART
page 264

IF YOU WANT THE OUTSIDE OF THE CHALLAH TO STAY PINK EVEN WHEN BAKED, COVER THE TOP OF THE CHALLAH LOOSELY WITH TIN FOIL AFTER THE FIRST 10 MINUTES OF BAKING.

STRAWBERRY SHORTCAKE CHALLAH

YIELD: 4 X 1LB CHALLAHS
or **2 LARGE CHALLAHS**

Whether you shape it into a heart or just a regular challah shape, this is going to make someone swoon with delight! This is a fun challah to make for an anniversary or other celebration on Shabbat. Top the challah with dried strawberries and/or sprinkles, and take this to a whole 'nother level. Pass the whipped cream please!

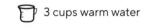 3 cups warm water

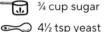 ¾ cup sugar

 4½ tsp yeast

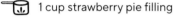 1 cup strawberry pie filling

 2 Tbsp oil

1 tsp clear vanilla extract (see notes)

 1 tsp butter flavoring (see notes)

 1½ Tbsp fine sea salt

 10-10½ cups all-purpose flour

Glaze:

1 white yolk, beaten with 2 tsp water

Topping:

Freeze-dried strawberries

White and pink sprinkles

Pearl sugar

1. Pour the **warm water** into a bowl. Add the **sugar** and **yeast**; stir to combine.

2. Add the **strawberry pie filling**, **oil**, **vanilla extract**, and **butter flavoring**; stir well.

3. Add the **salt** and **10 cups flour**, adding **remaining flour** as needed until the dough pulls away from the sides of the bowl.

4. Knead until smooth and elastic. Put a bit of oil in the challah bowl, and roll the dough around in it. Cover the bowl, and let rise in a warm spot for 1½-2 hours or overnight in the fridge.

5. When the dough is puffy, punch it down to let out the air, then do the challah separation without a blessing.*

6. Braid as desired, **glaze with egg**, and sprinkle with one (or a few) of the options listed!

7. Allow to rise for another 45-60 minutes, then bake in a 350°F oven for 30 minutes.

*SEE PAGE 27 FOR CHALLAH SEPARATION INSTRUCTIONS

RECIPE NOTES

♡ Find non-dairy butter flavoring at any baking supply store or online.

♡ Vanilla extract gives challah a bit of a yellowish tinge, so to get the pinkest pink, I suggest using a clear vanilla extract. But don't worry, if you use dark vanilla, it will still look great!

5-STRAND FISHTAIL WITH PEARL STRAND
page 263

GET CREATIVE AND DECORATE WITH ALL KINDS OF FUN SPRINKLES!

CUCKOO FOR COCOA CHOCOLATE CHALLAH

YIELD: 4 X 1LB CHALLAHS OR 2 LARGE CHALLAHS

It's chocolate, it's challah. Do you need any more convincing than that? If you really want to go crazy, make this recipe, the strawberry shortcake challah (*page 94*), and the birthday cake challah (*page 84*), then braid them all together to create a Neapolitan-style challah!
Talk about a showstopper.

2 cups warm water

½ cup sugar

¼ cup vanilla sugar

4½ tsp yeast

½ cup oil

2 eggs

2 tsp vanilla extract

½ cup cocoa powder

1½ Tbsp fine sea salt

6-6½ cups all-purpose flour

1 cup mini chocolate chips, optional

Glaze:
1 egg yolk, beaten with 2 tsp water

1. Pour the **warm water** into a bowl. Add the **sugar**, **vanilla sugar**, and **yeast**; stir to combine.

2. Add the **oil**, **eggs**, and **vanilla**; stir well.

3. Add the **cocoa powder**, **salt** and **6 cups flour**, adding the remaining flour as needed until the dough pulls away from the sides of the bowl.

4. Knead until smooth and elastic, then add the **chocolate chips** (if desired), and gently knead to incorporate.

5. Put a bit of oil in the challah bowl, and roll the dough around in it. Cover the bowl, and let rise in a warm spot for 1½-2 hours, or overnight in the fridge.

6. When the dough is puffy, punch it down to let out the air*.

7. Braid, then **glaze with egg**. Allow to rise for another 1-1½ hours, then bake in a 350°F oven for 35 minutes.

*NO CHALLAH SEPARATION REQUIRED, SEE PAGE 27 FOR DETAILS

HAPPY CHALLAH-DAYS!

CHALLAH
for THE
HOLIDAYS

CHALLAH FOR THE HOLIDAYS

Throughout the year, the Jewish calendar is filled with "Holy Days" or, Holidays!
Some of these holy days were given to us directly from Hashem in the Torah,
such as Rosh Hashanah, Yom Kippur, Sukkot, Pesach and Shavuot.
Some of our holidays started because of a special event in our history,
which our Sages wanted us to remember for all time, such as Purim and Chanukah.

The holidays that we were instructed to keep in the Torah,
are very similar to Shabbat in the way we observe them.
We light candles to welcome in the holiday, and create a warm ambience.
We eat special meals that begin with the Kiddush made over wine,
and the Hamotzi made over the challah.

Here is a collection of recipes that represent the meaning and flavors of each of the holidays.

Make them for the holidays, or maybe just make them for fun anytime!

Either way, I hope you enjoy these recipes
and make them a part of your Shabbat and holiday celebrations.

Happy Challah-Days!

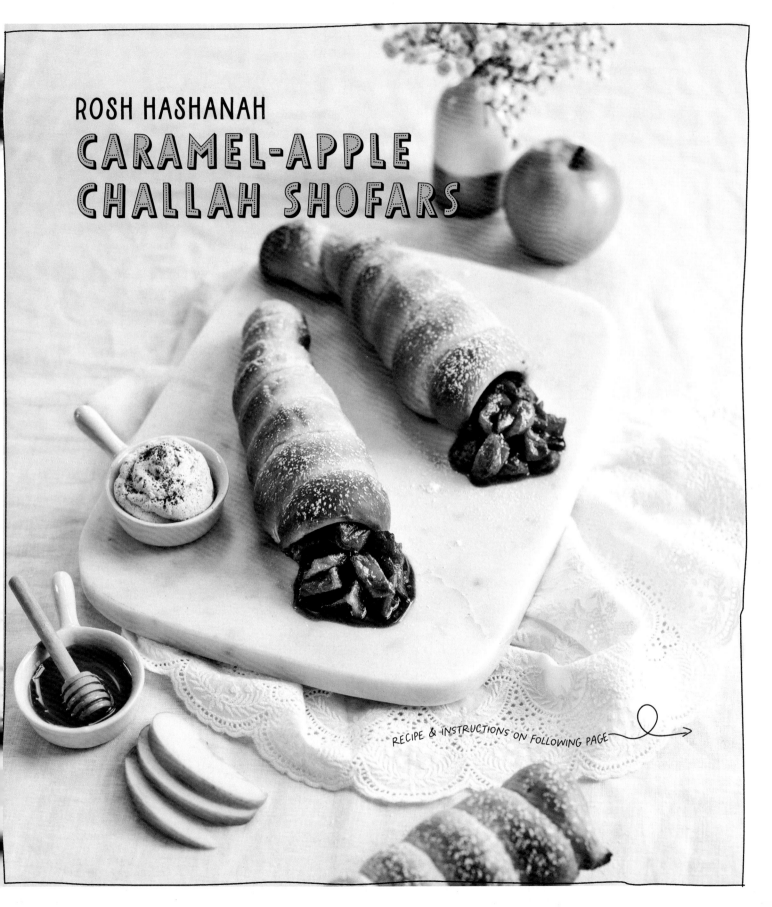

ROSH HASHANAH
CARAMEL-APPLE
CHALLAH SHOFARS

RECIPE & INSTRUCTIONS ON FOLLOWING PAGE

ROSH HASHANAH

CARAMEL-APPLE CHALLAH SHOFARS

YIELD: 6 SHOFARS

The traditional Rosh Hashanah challah is a round one, and is typically filled with raisins. We create a spiral to remind us of the cycle of the year, and how we grow each time we go around the sun again. And the raisins? To bring in more sweetness. So, here's a whole different take on the sweet spiral! We spiral the dough into the shape of the shofar that we blow on Rosh Hashanah, and then stuff it with caramelized apples (like the apples that we dip into honey on the holiday). You can come up with your own ideas of what to stuff these edible shofars with. You can even go savory with a yummy meat mixture or a salad. However you stuff it, this is a creative way to have your shofar and eat it too!

Equipment:

Cream horn molds,* or ice cream cones wrapped in foil

Large skillet

Shofar Ingredients:

24 oz challah dough

Glaze:

1 egg yolk, beaten with 2 tsp water

CARMELIZED APPLE:

2 Tbsp margarine

2 medium Granny Smith apples, finely diced (about 3 cups)

1 cup brown sugar

Juice of ½ lemon (about 1 Tbsp juice)

1 Tbsp cinnamon

1 tsp vanilla extract

CINNAMON WHIPPED CREAM:

1 cup non-dairy whipping cream

1 tsp ground cinnamon

*YOU CAN FIND INEXPENSIVE STAINLESS STEEL CREAM HORN MOLDS AT BED BATH & BEYOND OR OTHER HOUSEWARES STORES.

THE SHOFARS:

CARAMEL APPLE STUFFING:

1 Preheat the oven to 375°F. Lightly grease the outside of six cream horn molds or foil-wrapped ice cream cones. Divide dough into 6 (4 oz) portions, then roll each into a long, thin rope.

2 Starting at the wider end of the cone, wrap the rope around the entire mold, pinching off any extra dough if necessary. Glaze with egg, then bake upright on a baking sheet for 15 minutes. Allow to cool.

1 Melt the margarine in a large skillet over medium heat. Add the apples, brown sugar, lemon juice, cinnamon, and vanilla. Cook over medium heat, stirring occasionally, until apples are softened and liquid is syrupy, about 20 minutes in total. Remove from heat, and allow to cool completely.

2 Prepare the whipped cream: Beat whipping cream and cinnamon at medium speed until stiff peaks form.

3 When the challah shofars are completely cooled, stuff with the caramelized apple mixture, and serve with whipped cream on the side. Alternatively, fill challah shofars with cream, and serve with caramelized apples on the side.

SUKKOT IS CELEBRATED IN THE FALL. IT IS A TIME TO CELEBRATE THE HARVEST AND TO REMEMBER THAT WE ARE ALL UNITED UNDER HASHEM'S GREAT SUKKAH. SHAKING THE LULAV AND ETROG IS A SPECIAL MITZVAH OF SUKKOT AND THIS CHALLAH, LONG, LEAFY, AND FILLED WITH ALL THE YUMMY HERBS, REMINDS US OF THE LULAV.

★☆☆

SUKKOT

'EPI' HERB CHALLAH

EGG-FREE

YIELD: 2 EPI CHALLAHS

This shape of bread is known in French as epi, meaning ears of grain, and it creates a loaf that resembles a French baguette; the "ears of grain" become little pull-apart rolls. What a fun and delicious way to eat your challah!

Ingredients:

 ¼ cup fresh herbs, such as rosemary, thyme, sage, chives, and oregano, finely chopped

 2 lb Water Challah dough (*page 64*)

Topping:

All-purpose flour

Olive oil

Coarse sea salt

1 Preheat the oven to 400°F. Knead the herbs into the dough.

2 Divide the dough into two equal portions, tucking the ends under while rolling to create a tall baguette shape.

3 Place dough on a parchment-lined baking sheet. Sprinkle a generous amount of flour on top.

4 Holding your scissors at a 45° angle, make deep-angled cuts from side to side, almost to the bottom.

5 Drizzle with olive oil, then sprinkle with coarse salt. Allow to rise for about 30 minutes, then bake for 25 minutes.

JELLY

CUSTARD

EATING DEEP FRIED FOOD ON CHANUKAH REMINDS US OF THE MIRACLE OF THE OIL IN THE MENORAH, WHICH IS A GREAT EXCUSE TO EAT DOUGHNUTS! HERE'S AN ORIGINAL TWIST ON THE TRADITIONAL SUFGANIYOT, WHICH IS HEBREW FOR DOUGHNUTS.

CHANUKAH
SUFGANIYOT FRIES

YIELD: APPROXIMATELY 18 DOUGHNUT FRIES

WARNING: THIS RECIPE USES HOT OIL, AND REQUIRES ADULT SUPERVISION

Ingredients:

Oil, for frying
(such as canola or peanut)

32 oz Classic Challah dough (*page 56*) or Brioche dough (*page 68*)

Confectioners' sugar,
for sprinkling

Serve with:

Jelly and/or custard

1 Roll dough into a large (roughly 6x18-inch) rectangle, about ½-inch thick. Using a pizza cutter, cut dough into 1-inch wide strips.

2 Heat oil halfway in a medium pot over high heat. You'll know it's ready when a small piece of dough inserted into the oil begins to sizzle.

3 You're ready to start frying! Prepare a wire cooling rack, or line a tray with paper towels. Deep fry the dough strips for 6-8 seconds on each side. Don't crowd the pot — there should be plenty of room for all the strips to float to the top. Carefully remove from oil using a slotted spoon or tongs.

4 Drain on the prepared cooling rack. Dust with confectioners' sugar while still warm. Serve with jelly or custard.

TU B'SHVAT
GARDEN FOCACCIA

YIELD: 1 FOCACCIA

*LOTS TO DO FOR
THE LITTLEST HANDS!*

Ingredients:

 16-24 oz Water Challah
dough (*page 64*)

Topping:
*GET CREATIVE AND USE YOUR
FAVORITES!*

Cherry tomatoes

Black olives

Chives or scallions

Herbs such as: dill, parsley,
cilantro, sage, rosemary

Mini peppers

Red onions or shallots

Thin asparagus spears

Radishes

Olives

Garlic cloves

Pepitas or sunflower seeds

Olive oil, for drizzling

Finishing salt,
such as Maldon

1 Prepare the vegetable
decorations, by cutting
them into pretty shapes; set
aside until you're ready to
decorate.

2 Roll the dough to fit into
a parchment-lined or well
greased half-size baking
sheet. Allow to rise until puffy,
30-45 minutes.

3 Using your fingers, push deep
into the dough to make little
wells. Drizzle the olive oil
generously all over the dough.
Sprinkle with some finishing
salt.

4 Decorate the focaccia using
the prepared vegetables.
Generously drizzle olive oil all
over. Bake in a 425°F oven for
20 minutes, until the focaccia
is golden.

On Purim we eat three-cornered cookies stuffed with a variety of yummy fillings, called hamentashen. Here is the challah take on that! Get creative with different doughs, toppings, and fillings throughout the book to create new, unique hamentashen flavor combinations.

Try the Maple Challah dough (*page 86*) with a pecan pie filling (*page 214*) for a sweet version.
What about the Italian Herb Challah dough (*page 88*) with a garlic filling (*page 235*) for a savory version?

CHOCOLATE-PEANUT BUTTER

Cuckoo for Cocoa Chocolate Challah (*page 96*)
+
Store bought chocolate hazelnut spread
+
Peanut Butter Glaze (*page 229*)

LOTUS™ INSANITY

Gingerbread Challah (*page 80*)
+
Store bought cookie butter (like Lotus™)
+
Lotus™ Crumble (*page 230*)

LEMON POPPY

Lemon Poppy Challah (*page 78*)
+
Sweet Poppy Filling (*page 235*)
+
Lemon Glaze (*page 229*)

Glaze:

1 egg yolk, beaten with 2 tsp water

MY OWN CREATIONS:

_____ + _____ + _____

_____ + _____ + _____

_____ + _____ + _____

PURIM

CHALLAH-TASHEN 3 WAYS

CHOCOLATE-PEANUT BUTTER

LOTUS™ INSANITY

LEMON POPPY

HAPPY PURIM from the Pinsons

Instructions:

1. Preheat the oven to 350°F.

2. Use about 1½ oz dough per hamentashen. Roll out each ball of dough into a circle, or flatten with your fingers.

3. Place a rounded heaping teaspoon of filling in the center. Gather up the edges, and pinch very tightly together. Unlike cookie hamentashen, these challah hamentashen should be completely sealed up, as they may open or spread a bit during baking to reveal the inside!

4. Glaze with egg (if making the Lotus Insanity, top with crunch topping before baking). Bake for 20 minutes.

5. Allow to cool completely, then glaze (peanut butter glaze for the chocolate PB version, and lemon glaze for the lemon poppy version).

DID YOU KNOW?

SOME SAY THAT HAMENTASHEN STARTED OFF AS A DESSERT CALLED A "MOHN TASH" (MOHN MEANING POPPY IN YIDDISH) OR "POPPY POCKET," WHICH WAS A COMMON PASTRY AT THE TIME, AND SOME CLEVER PERSON NAMED IT A "HA-MOHN TASH" AFTER THE WICKED HAMAN IN THE PURIM STORY... AND THE REST IS HISTORY!

111

POST-PESACH MUFLETA

MOROCCAN MIMOUNA CHALLAH

THIS RECIPE REQUIRES ADULT SUPERVISION

My first challah cookbook, *Rising! The Book of Challah*, also had a challah for every holiday, except of course, the holiday of Pesach. I say of course, because the main thing we do on Pesach is stay away from things that rise! We don't eat anything with yeast that can rise, and of course, the main thing we abstain from is bread and challah!

But as I learned more about the challah traditions of each Jewish culture, I found that there was in fact a special challah that is made as soon as Pesach ends! It is a time when we pray for a blessing for the grains, and the Moroccan community makes a huge celebration called Mimouna, which is full of sweets and treats that use all the stuff we don't eat on Pesach. The special bread of that celebration is a dough that is spread into a thin pancake, fried, stacked high, and served with butter and honey.

Ingredients:

 3½ cups warm water

 2 heaping Tbsp sugar

1 Tbsp yeast

 6½ cups all-purpose flour

 1½ tsp fine sea salt

Oil, (for your hands and counter)

Topping:

Melted butter (optional)

Honey

1. Pour the **warm water** into a bowl. Add the **sugar** and **yeast**; stir to combine.

2. Add **3 cups flour**; mix well. Add the **salt** and **remaining flour**, and knead just until the dough pulls away from the sides of the bowl. The dough will be very wet (looser than a regular challah dough), which is the way it should be. Make sure your hands are oiled a bit when kneading to prevent adding too much flour.

3. Put a bit of **oil** in the challah bowl, and roll the dough around in it. Cover the bowl, and let it rise in a warm spot for 40 minutes.

4. When the dough is puffy, punch it down to let out the air.*

5. See the following page for step-by-step shaping and frying instructions.

*NO CHALLAH SEPARATION REQUIRED, SEE PAGE 27 FOR DETAILS

STEP-BY-STEP INSTRUCTIONS ON FOLLOWING PAGE

Now let's shape it and fry it!

1 Tear off balls of dough, roughly 3½ oz each. Working one at a time, shape into a smooth ball, ensuring that the remaining dough is covered in the meantime.

2 Brush a smooth surface (such as a clean countertop or cutting board) with a bit of oil, and oil your fingertips as well. Press the dough into a very thin, flat pancake, approximately 7-8 inches across.

3 Preheat a non-stick skillet over medium heat. Using your hands, lift the pancake by the edges, and place flat into the skillet. Cook for less than a minute or until golden, then flip and cook on the other side for less than a minute or until golden.

4 While the first pancake is cooking, flatten another ball of dough (step 1). Once the first pancake is cooked on both sides, place a second pancake on top of it in the skillet. Flip with a spatula, and cook the second pancake for less than a minute or until golden. Flatten a third pancake, and place it on top. Flip, cook, and repeat. Only the first pancake will be cooked on both sides. The rest of the stack cooks only on one side each.

5 Drizzle with melted butter and honey, and serve mufleta while still warm.

LAG B'OMER
S'MORES CHALLAH

Lag B'omer is a day that celebrates the *tzadik* called the "Rashbi" and his great contribution to uncovering the mysteries of the Torah. We celebrate by making bonfires and singing around the fire. Since we're already outside and lighting fires, we might as well make it a BBQ, which has become a very common tradition on Lag B'Omer. If it's a BBQ, you know there has to be s'mores. And if I'm going to make it, it has to be challah! So here it is — the s'mores challah.
WOW!

RECIPE AND INSTRUCTIONS ON FOLLOWING PAGE

LAG B'OMER
S'MORES CHALLAH

YIELD: 6 PULL-APART

Ingredients:

20-24 oz challah dough of choice

3½ oz bar of dark chocolate

12 marshmallows

Glaze:

1 egg yolk, beaten with 2 tsp water

Topping:

Graham Cracker S'mores Crunch
(*page 230*)

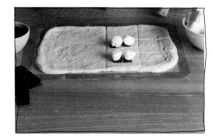

1 Roll the **dough** into a large 16-inch rectangle. Score the dough in half, then score 6 even squares on that half of the dough.

2 Top each section with **two squares of chocolate**, and top each square of chocolate with **half of a marshmallow**. Bring the other side of the dough over the chocolate and marshmallows.

3 Line an 8-inch baking pan with parchment paper. Using a bench scraper or sharp knife, cut the dough into squares, pinch the edges shut, and place onto the prepared baking pan. Cover and allow to rise for about 30 minutes, until puffy.

4 **Glaze the dough with egg**, then top with the **graham cracker topping**. Bake in a 350°F oven for 25-30 minutes. Allow to cool before eating, since the chocolate inside gets VERY hot. Pull apart and enjoy!

SHAVUOT
CHEESE FLOWERS

RECIPE AND INSTRUCTIONS ON FOLLOWING PAGE

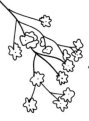

★☆☆
SHAVUOT
CHEESE FLOWERS

YIELD: 8-12 CHEESE FLOWERS

Shavuot is the day we received the Torah and became the Jewish nation. The Torah was given to us on Mount Sinai, a small mountain in the middle of the desert, surrounded by much bigger and more impressive mountains. But this little humble mountain was chosen to teach us the lesson that the littlest people we may not even notice, can do the very biggest things!

Mount Sinai was a plain mountain, not beautiful in any way, but because it was chosen by Hashem to do something so important, it suddenly became the most beautiful mountain in all the desert, miraculously blooming into a glorious flower-filled expanse. We remember this by decorating our homes and synagogues with flowers on Shavuot. Another great tradition of Shavuot is to eat dairy (and challah of course)! I've combined all these ideas—flowers, cheese and challah—and came up with this recipe — a beautiful, delicious treat for Shavuot breakfast, dessert, or anytime we want to remember this message of Mount Sinai—*that little people can do important things!*

Ingredients:

24-36 oz Classic Challah dough (*page 56*)
or Brioche dough (*page 68*)

Cheese Filling:

 1 egg yolk

8 ounces cream cheese, softened

¼ cup confectioners' sugar

1 tsp lemon juice

¼ tsp vanilla extract

Glaze:

1 egg yolk, beaten with 2 tsp water

Topping:

Pearl sugar or Belgian waffle sugar

Confectioners' sugar

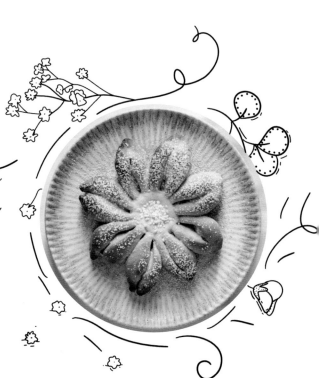

1
Preheat the oven to 350°F. Using an electric mixer, beat **egg yolk**, **cream cheese**, **confectioners' sugar**, **lemon juice**, and **vanilla extract** on medium-high speed until smooth. Keep in the fridge until ready to use.

2
Divide the **dough** into 8-12 (3 oz) portions; roll into balls.

3
Press the bottom of a small glass into the center of each ball, then use a paring knife or bench scraper to cut 10 slices around.

4
Pinch 2 slices together to form a petal; repeat with remaining slices to form 5 petals in total for each flower. Place flowers on a parchment-lined baking sheet.

5
Glaze with egg, then top with 1 heaping tablespoon of **cream cheese filling** in the center. Cover lightly and allow to rise for about 25-30 minutes, or until puffy.

6
Sprinkle some **pearl sugar** on top of the cream cheese filling. Bake for 25 minutes. Dust with **confectioners' sugar** before serving.

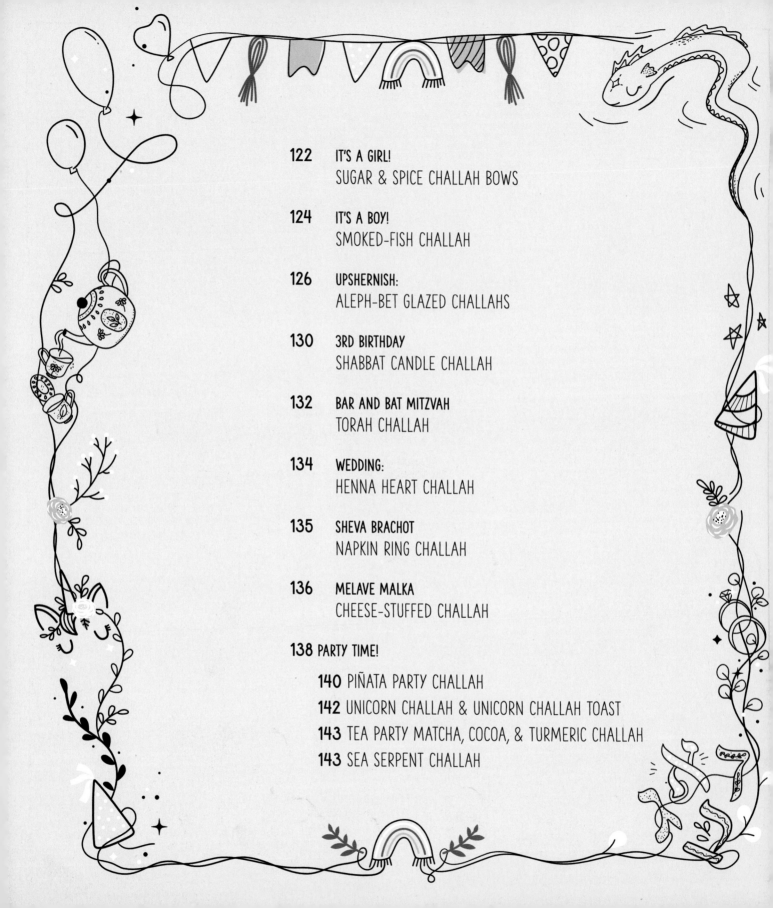

CHALLAH FOR LIFE'S SPECIAL OCCASIONS

CELEBRATION CHALLAHS

PAREVE *or* DAIRY

IT'S A GIRL!

SUGAR & SPICE CHALLAH BOWS

YIELD: 6 CHALLAH BOWS

"SUGAR AND SPICE AND EVERYTHING NICE, THAT'S WHAT LITTLE GIRLS ARE MADE OF!"
For a new baby girl's first Shabbat, or for the *"kiddush"* to celebrate the birth of a new baby girl, what could be cuter than these little challah bows? For the extra wow factor, decorate them with some pretty pink sparkles or dragées, or tie a ribbon around them! *Either way, whoever receives these adorable challahs will be tickled pink!*

1 cup sugar

¼ cup cinnamon

2 tsp ground cloves

¼ tsp nutmeg

¼ medium recipe Classic Challah dough (*page 56*) (about 24 oz), or other sweet dough (such as Strawberry Shortcake challah (page 94; as pictured below)

½ cup (1 stick) margarine or butter, melted

Glaze:
1 egg white, beaten with 2 tsp water

1. Mix **sugar**, **cinnamon**, **ground cloves**, and **nutmeg**; set aside.

2. Divide the **dough** into 12 equal portions, then roll each ball into a flat circle.

3. Brush the top of each dough circle with **melted margarine**, then sprinkle a generous amount of the **cinnamon-sugar** mixture on top. Cover with a second dough circle. Repeat to create six stacks.

4. Proceed to shape the bows as pictured.

Cut 1 slit in the top of the circle, and 2 slits on the bottoms.

Fold over from the top to the bottom, creating a bow shape.

Take the "tab" on the bottom and wrap it around the center.

Allow to rise for 20 min., glaze with egg and decorate as desired. Bake at 350°F for 15-20 minutes.

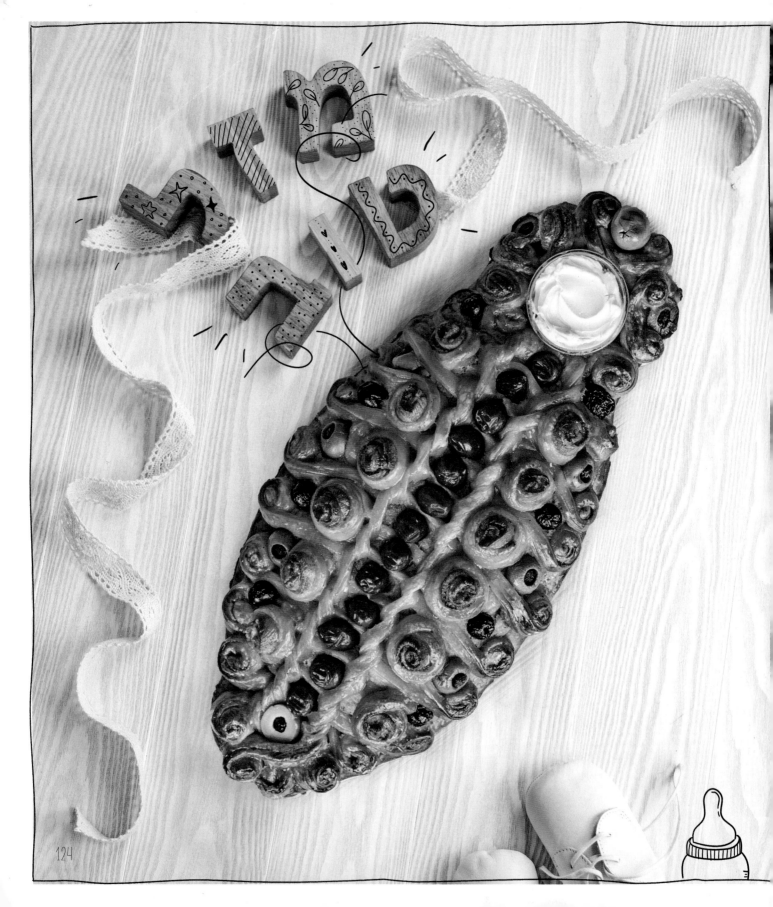

★★★

IT'S A BOY!
SMOKED-FISH CHALLAH

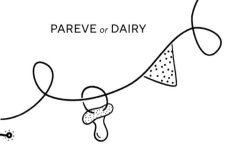

YIELD: 1 LARGE CENTERPIECE CHALLAH

Have you ever been to a bris? If so, you probably noticed smoked fish somewhere on the buffet. There's also usually either challah or bagels, being that it's a *Seudat Mitzvah*, a feast for a mitzvah, which always involves washing for bread. Here I've combined the two into a smoked fish platter that is stuffed with fish, shaped like a fish, but made out of challah! *How cool is that?* Best of all, it's really yummy.

Ingredients:

 1 medium recipe Classic Challah dough (*page 56*)

 2 cups smoked whitefish spread

 ½ cup breadcrumbs

All-purpose flour, for dusting

10-12 oz sliced lox

Glaze:

1 egg yolk, beaten with 2 tsp water

Topping:

Cherry tomatoes

Pitted black olives

Sliced green olives

DID YOU KNOW?

THE MITZVAH IS TO DO THE BRIS ON THE 8TH DAY, SO IN ORDER TO SHOW OUR LOVE FOR HASHEM AND THE MITZVOT, WE TRY TO DO IT AS SOON AS POSSIBLE, WHICH IS WHY IT'S USUALLY EARLY IN THE MORNING!

Let's make it!

1. Divide the **dough** into 2 equal portions — one for the base of the fish and one for the top.

2. Mix the **whitefish spread** and **breadcrumbs**; set aside.

3. Roll out one of the pieces for the base into a large (21x17-inch) rectangle.

4. Using a pizza cutter, cut out an oblong fish shape (without a tail), then place on a parchment-lined baking sheet. Reserve the cuts for later to use for the curlicues around the tail.

5. Mound the **whitefish mixture** onto the **dough**, leaving plenty of space around the edges. Set aside.

6. Roll out the second piece of **dough** into a large rectangle, about ¼-inch thick.

7. Using a small oven rack, score lines into the dough. This will help achieve even strips.

8. Using a pizza cutter or bench scraper, cut about 16 strips of dough along the scored lines.

9. Create a loop in the center of the first strip, and pull the next strip through. Dust with flour, if needed, to ensure the dough doesn't stick.

126

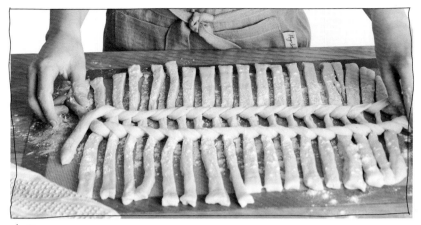

10 Repeat until completed.

11 Carefully lift the "crocheted" rectangle, place directly on top of the whitefish-topped dough. Get some help for this step!

Curl the ends of each dough strip, then place a rolled up **strip of lox** in between each one. Place **cherry tomatoes** in the holes in the center, and decorate with **olives**. Use the extra bits of dough from step 4 to create curlicues around an oven-proof bowl (which can be filled with cream cheese or sour cream once baked). Use a strip to create a mouth, then finish with a **black olive** as the eye.

13 **Glaze with egg**. Allow to rise for 30 minutes, then bake in a 350°F oven for 25-30 minutes. Allow to cool on a cooling rack, then carefully transfer to a large platter or board. Fill the bowl with **cream cheese** or **sour cream**.

★☆☆
ALEPH-BET GLAZED CHALLAHS

There is a Jewish custom to allow a boy's hair to grow until the age of three. On his third birthday there is a celebration called the "*Upshernish*" in Yiddish, or "*Tisporet*" in Hebrew, meaning haircut. At the *Upshernish*, the birthday boy's long hair is cut, while being careful to leave some hair at the side of the ears called the "*peyot*" (sidelocks). This marks the beginning of his education as a Jewish child, and the custom is to sweeten the Hebrew letters (sometimes with honey) to introduce the child to the sweetness of Torah.

Ingredients:

1 medium recipe Classic Challah dough
(*page 56*)

Topping:

Icing Glaze of choice (*page 229*)

1. Preheat the oven to 350°F. Divide dough into 2½-3 oz portions per letter. Roll each portion into a log, then shape into desired letters of the Aleph Beis. Place letters on a parchment-lined baking sheet.

2. Allow to rise for about 20-30 minutes, but not too long or the letters will lose their shape.

3. Bake in a 350°F oven for 12-15 minutes. Allow to cool completely before glazing. After glazing, keep each letter separate until the glaze hardens completely.

RECIPE NOTES:
Serve within a day of making. If baking in advance of the celebrations, freeze the letters and glaze before serving.

CAN YOU NAME ALL THE LETTERS OF THE HEBREW ALEPH-BET?

The beautiful wooden letters featured in this book are handmade by Denebeims, and can be purchased online.

★★☆

3RD BIRTHDAY

SHABBAT CANDLE CHALLAH

Just as there is a custom for introducing a boy into his Jewish education, some people have a custom that a Jewish girl lights her very own Shabbat candle at three years old, to mark the beginning of her learning and observance of the Torah and *Mitzvot*.

It is customary to get the birthday girl her very own candlestick, and some even make a ceremony to celebrate the special occasion of her very first time lighting a candle for Shabbat.

A beautiful idea to mark this special time is to create a Shabbat candlestick made from challah to serve for the birthday girl's first candle-lighting Shabbat!

Go ahead and get creative, there are no rules or instructions here — just take some challah dough and play around with the shapes and braids. You can glaze it after it cools, just like the challah aleph-bet letters on the previous page, or you can top it with pretty sprinkles or fun toppings.

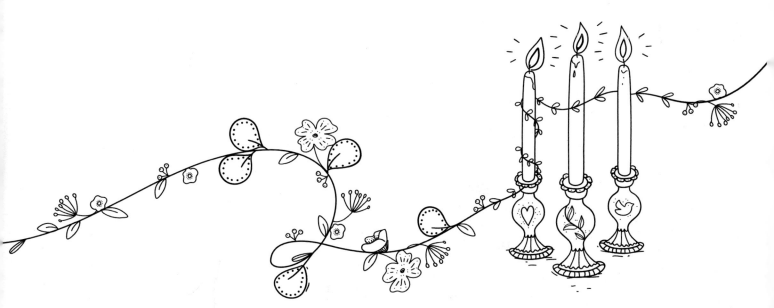

SIDES OF TORAH: SIX- OR SEVEN- STRAND WEAVE
page 267 or page 269
HANDLES: ONE-STRAND TWIST
page 258

מזל טוב

BAR AND BAT MITZVAH
TORAH CHALLAH

When a girl turns 12 and a boy turns 13, they are considered inheritors of the Torah's traditions and obligated to observe the mitzvot, thereby becoming *"B'nei Mitzvah"* (children of the *mitzvot*). Sometimes the Bar and Bat Mitzvah parties get so crazy, it becomes more about the "bar" than the *mitzvah*! But this challah will remind everyone what this celebration is truly about — taking on the responsibility of being a part of the Jewish people and being a letter in the Torah scroll of our history. That's a big deal, and it deserves a special challah to mark the occasion!

This challah is a combination of two large flat-weave challahs and one piece of dough rolled out for the "parchment." All are baked separately, then assembled.

Ingredients:

 1 medium recipe Classic Challah dough (*page 56*)

Egg Glaze:

1 egg yolk, beaten with 2 tsp water

Toppings:

Seeds, as desired

Instructions:

1. Divide challah dough into 7 portions:
   - 1 portion should be about 8-10 oz (for the parchment of the Torah scroll).
   - 2 of the portions should be about 30 oz each (for the sides of the Torah scroll).
   - 4 small portions should be about 3 oz each (for the Torah handles).

2. Line two baking sheets with parchment paper. For the parchment of the Torah scroll, roll the 8-10 oz piece into a large rectangle. Place on one of the baking sheets.

3. For the sides of the Torah scroll, divide the 30 oz pieces into as many strands as you need,

then braid into two six- or seven- strand weave challahs. Place on the second baking sheet.

4. For the handles, roll the 3 oz pieces into long strands, then twist from the center point of the strand. Place the handles on the top and bottom of each challah.

5. Once the flat piece of dough (the parchment) has started to puff up a bit, poke a few holes in it to let out the air, then bake in a 350°F oven (without glaze) until lightly golden brown, about 12-15 minutes. Allow to cool.

6. When the challahs and handles are nice and puffy, brush with egg glaze. Add seeds or toppings as desired. Bake for 35-45 minutes. Allow to cool, then transfer to a serving tray, and assemble as pictured.

7. As a final touch, you can paint anything you'd like on the "parchment," such as the words "Mazal Tov" and maybe the name of the boy or girl who is lucky enough to have this challah for their celebration.

(See page 254 for instructions on painting a challah.)

WEDDING
HENNA HEART CHALLAH

The Henna (or Cheena) ceremony is a Sephardic tradition that celebrates an upcoming wedding by decorating the kallah (bride) and guests with painted henna designs. Everyone comes wearing elaborate traditional costumes and headdresses.

Of course I've transferred that beautiful idea to challah. It is a beautiful gift to present to the bride for the Shabbat before her wedding, or perhaps as a special challah for the wedding itself!

PAINTING ON CHALLAH, *page 244*
WOVEN HEART CHALLAH, *page 273*

★ ☆ ☆

SHEVA BRACHOT
NAPKIN-RING CHALLAH

For a whole week after a Jewish wedding, the bride and groom are celebrated with seven feasts hosted by family and friends. We make a blessing on challah, and then after the meal we say seven special blessings to honor the new couple. Here's a creative and beautiful way to serve individual challah portions, while weaving it into the tablescape decor!

THIS IS A REAL, EDIBLE CHALLAH!

CHALLAH NAPKIN RING, *page 271*

Ingredients:

- 8 Tbsp (1 stick) unsalted butter
- 2 Tbsp chopped garlic*
- ¾ tsp fine sea salt
- 1 Tbsp finely chopped fresh parsley
- 1 finely diced jalapeño or 1 tsp red chili flakes, optional
- 1 crusty loaf water challah
- 1 cup shredded mozzarella or cheddar cheese (or both)

*Use store bought pre-chopped garlic to make this recipe super easy!

STUFFING THE CHEESE INTO THE CRACKS OF THE CHALLAH IS A SUPER FUN JOB FOR LITTLE HANDS!

★★☆

MELAVE MALKA
CHEESE-STUFFED CHALLAH

Shabbat is so precious to us that we don't want to just let her go without a grand goodbye. *Melave Malka* means "to accompany the queen," and we prepare a party after Shabbat, on Saturday night, as our farewell to the Shabbat Queen. It's usually a dairy meal, as we've had our share of meat on Shabbat! So here's a fun *Melave Malka* treat. *The Shabbat Queen is never going to want to leave this party!*

1 Preheat the oven to 350°F.
Add **butter**, **garlic**, and **salt** to a microwave-safe bowl, and melt for 30 seconds in the microwave. Alternatively, melt in a saucepan over medium heat.

2 Add the **parsley** and **jalapeño** or **red chili flakes** (if desired).

3 Place the **challah** on a large piece of foil (big enough for the sides to cover the challah). Cut the top of the challah on the bias into 1-inch diamonds, making sure not to cut all the way through.

4 Using your fingers, pry open each crack, and drizzle the **melted butter** mixture all over. Stuff each crevice with **cheese**. This doesn't need to be super neat — it's nice to have some of the butter and cheese all over the crust.

5 Bring the sides of the foil over to cover the challah. Bake for 20 minutes, then unwrap and bake for another 5-10 minutes until crusty and oozing cheese. Serve immediately.

137

★★☆

PIÑATA

PARTY
CHALLAH

PIÑATA PARTY CHALLAH

RECIPE AND INSTRUCTIONS ON FOLLOWING PAGE

It's a challah.
It's also like a piñata since it's stuffed with candies.
On the outside it looks like a birthday gift - which is totally adorable as it is.
But then tear open this challah and watch their jaws drop when piles of candies come spilling out of this crazy challah!
Someone is about to have a very happy birthday!

Ingredients:

24 oz Classic Challah dough (*page 56*) or Brioche dough (*page 68*)

Decorative dough (*page 255*)

Glaze:

1 egg yolk, beaten with 2 tsp water

Topping:

Colored sprinkles

Colorful sanding sugar

Candies to stuff into the challah piñata

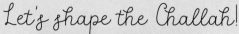

Let's shape the Challah!

1 Divide the dough into 4 (6 oz) portions. Roll each portion into a flat circle, then fold in the edges to form a square.

2 Place the dough squares into a greased pan. Glaze with egg, then decorate with colored sprinkles. Cover lightly with a dish towel, and allow to rise until nice and puffy.

MAKE THE BOW!

4 Using the 2 wide strips, fold as pictured, then loop the small piece of dough around it to form a bow.

5 Gently decorate the challah with the strips as pictured, laying the ribbon in a criss-cross pattern over the gaps between the challah squares.

3

Roll out decorative dough. Using a pizza cutter, slice 4 short strips for the ribbons, 2 wider strips for the bow, and a small piece of dough to wrap around the bow. Glaze pieces with egg, then decorate with colorful sanding sugar.

6

Top with the bow.
Bake in a 350°F oven for 30-35 minutes.
Allow to cool completely before stuffing the piñata.

Let's stuff it!

1 Once challah is completely cooled, use a sharp knife to carefully cut around the bow in the center of the challah. Remove the bow and the challah under it; set aside for later.

2 Place the challah on the tray that you will serve it on (not pictured). Fill the hole with all of your favorite candies.

3 Cover the hole with the bow. Shhhh... your secret is safe with me! Wait and see the surprise on everyone's faces when you cut into this magical challah!

141

★★☆ DAIRY or PAREVE

FANTASY PARTY
UNICORN CHALLAH
& Unicorn Challah Toast

1. Cut **challah** into slices, then toast (if desired).
2. Mix **cream cheese** and **food coloring**, using a different bowl for each color.
3. "Paint" your toasted challah slices with the colorful cream cheeses, then decorate with **sprinkles**!

1. See page 254 for instructions on coloring your dough. Knead food coloring of choice into the amount of dough you want to use for a unicorn challah.
2. Braid into a 5-strand top twist (see page 264 for instructions), then twist the top and bottom of the braid to create the shape of the unicorn's mane.
3. Allow to rise, then glaze with beaten egg white. Bake as is, or top with some unicorn-inspired sprinkles.
Prepare for some major oohs and ahhs!

DID YOU KNOW?

UNICORNS ARE IN THE TORAH!
During the building of the *mishkan* (the traveling Temple) in the desert, we were instructed by Hashem to use the skin of the *tachash* animal. Our Sages described the *tachash* as a desert animal with a gorgeous multicolor skin and one horn in the middle of its head (sounds like a unicorn!). The *tachash* appeared when the *mishkan* was being built, then vanished, *and was never seen again!*

TEA PARTY
MATCHA, COCOA & TURMERIC CHALLAH

DID YOU KNOW?
In the story of creation in the Torah, it says that Hashem created the "great sea monster" called the *tannin*. It also speaks in the Torah of the "*leviathan*," a giant fish or sea creature. So sea serpents are in the Torah too!

1. Follow steps to make Classic Challah (*page 56*), but divide the challah dough into 3 parts before kneading. At this point the dough should be very sticky (don't add all of the flour).
2. Add **2 Tbsp turmeric** to the first portion of dough, **¼ cup cocoa powder** to the second portion, and **¼ cup matcha powder** to the third portion.
3. Knead each piece separately, adding a bit of flour as needed to achieve a cohesive dough.
4. Braid portions together. Glaze with **beaten egg white**, then sprinkle with **edible flower petals**, such as rose, lavender, and chamomile. Bake as directed.

SEA SERPENT CHALLAH

1. Knead **green food coloring** into the amount of **dough** you want to use for the sea serpent challah.
2. Braid into a 5-strand top twist (*see page 264 for instructions*)
3. Using a bench scraper or sharp knife, cut into one end of the braid, dividing it in half for the tail of the serpent. Point the ends of the tails.
4. Glaze with **beaten egg white**, then cover the challah in **pepitas** (pumpkin seeds) for a scaled effect. Bake as directed.

CHALLAH FOR BREAKFAST, SNACK, LUNCH & DINNER

CHALLAH ALL DAY!

SWEET OR SAVORY
BELGIAN CHALLAH WAFFLES

Did you know that the famous Belgian waffles, which have become so popular,
are not really Belgian waffles at all?

One of the hallmarks of a Belgian waffle is the deep grooves in the waffle iron, which make the waffle extra
crispy on the outside. The American take on the Belgian waffle is just a standard American pancake or waffle
batter that is poured into a Belgian waffle maker.

But real Belgian waffles are not just about the deep grooves, they are actually made with a dough, not a batter.
A dough that is very much like a challah dough!

So, since I see the world through challah-colored glasses, I am very pleased to introduce you to my version
of the Jewish Belgian waffle, the Challah Waffle! This delicious waffle can be made using my classic challah
dough recipe, and you can go with the traditional crunchy sugar version for a sweet and delicious breakfast.

But don't stop there — it's not just for breakfast! I've also given you an option to make it savory, and these
waffles can act as bread for the most amazing sandwiches. Try topping it with schnitzel and a drizzle of maple
syrup, and you'll have a delicious take on the famous fried chicken and waffle sandwich, but Jewish challah
waffle style!

Happy Waffling!

RECIPE AND INSTRUCTIONS ON FOLLOWING PAGE

SWEET OR SAVORY
BELGIAN CHALLAH WAFFLES

YIELD: 10-12 WAFFLES

Belgian waffle irons have much deeper grooves, which is part of its distinct Belgian waffleness. If you only have a regular waffle iron, that will work too! These taste great the next day as well, just warm them up in the oven or even in a toaster! Fill with your favorite sandwich fixings or pour some syrup over it. *Enjoy*!

Ingredients:

32 oz Classic Challah dough (*page 56*)

For sweet Challah Waffles:

⅔ cup Belgian pearl sugar*

Confectioners' sugar, for serving

OR

For savory Challah Waffles:

⅔ cup crispy fried onions**

*   If you have a hard time finding Belgian pearl sugar in your local grocery store, it is readily available with kosher certification online.

** The most famous version of this product is made by French's™ and is certified kosher by OU. I also have a homemade version on page 233.

Your waffle questions answered:

The waffle maker is so much bigger than the waffle we're making. Is that a problem?

Belgian waffle irons are large, and these are smaller waffles, so they will only take up the center of the iron. But don't worry, they will still look beautiful once done.

How long do I keep the waffles in the waffle maker?

Use the first ball of dough to determine how long you need to keep them in. Each waffle iron has different settings and heats differently. You want the edges to be golden brown and crisp, but you don't want the inside to dry out. The waffles cook faster than you might think, so don't walk away!

Please be very careful!

Be careful when removing the waffles from the iron, especially if you went with the sweet pearl sugar option; the sugar on the surface gets very hot, and you can burn yourself easily. Ask an adult for help with this.

Let's make the waffles!

1 Roll the **dough** into a large (12-14") square. Generously sprinkle the entire surface with the **pearl sugar** or **crispy onions**.

2 Roll it up jelly roll-style! Grab a friend and do it together, it's a lot of fun!

3 Using a bench scraper or sharp knife, slice the log into 10-12 pieces.

4 Roll the pieces into balls, then cover and allow to rest for 15-20 minutes. You can make the waffles right away, or cover with plastic wrap and refrigerate overnight.

5 Heat the waffle iron, and spray it with a **cooking spray**. Place a ball of dough in the center of the griddle. Close, and cook until lightly golden brown; most waffle makers have an indicator light that will turn green once the waffle is cooked, but it should take anywhere from 2-4 minutes.

6 If you made the sweet version, dust with **confectioners' sugar**.

★★☆

CHALLAH CHURROS

YIELD: 16 CHALLAH CHURROS

I know, I know. Churros are dessert, not breakfast. But what if the churros were really innocent French toast sticks deep fried in a delicious bath, then covered up in a crunchy, sweet, and sticky blanket? Can we then count that as breakfast? I voted YES, and it was decided unanimously in favor of breakfast. (To be fair, I was the only one voting, but still!) So here it is, churros for breakfast. *You're welcome.*

Cinnamon Sugar
½ cup sugar & 1 Tbsp cinnamon mixed together

 1 large loaf day-old challah
 4 eggs
 ½ cup milk
 ¼ cup sugar
 2 tsp vanilla extract
 1 tsp cinnamon
 ½ tsp fine sea salt
 Oil, for frying

1 Cut off the crust of the **challah**, then square off the edges. Cut into four thick slices, then cut each slice into four sticks, about 1½-inches thick.

2 Whisk **eggs**, **milk**, **sugar**, **vanilla**, **cinnamon**, and **salt**. Heat about 2 inches of **oil** in a deep frying pan or saucepan.

3 Working in batches of about four at a time, dip challah sticks into the **egg mixture** until coated on all sides.

4 Once oil is hot and shimmering, fry coated challah sticks until golden brown.

5 Using tongs, transfer immediately to the prepared **cinnamon-sugar mixture**. Let cool on a wire cooling rack. Serve immediately with chocolate dipping sauce (next page).

151

★☆☆

SERVE WITH

CHOCOLATE DIPPING SAUCE

And yes, I still say this counts as breakfast.

Ingredients:

4 oz chocolate chips

½ cup heavy cream or non-dairy whipping cream

½ tsp vanilla extract

½ tsp cinnamon

Instructions:

1. Combine all ingredients in a microwave-safe bowl.

2. Microwave in 30-second increments, stirring after each one, until the chocolate is just melted.

BREAKFAST IN BED
CHALLAH EGG MUFFIN

*RECIPE AND INSTRUCTIONS
ON FOLLOWING PAGE*

CHALLAH EGG MUFFIN

YIELD: 6 EGG MUFFINS

Breakfast in bed for Mother's Day is a classic for a reason. But there's a dark truth about breakfast in bed... the Mom who wants to be treated like royalty early in the morning does not want to be the one who washes the bed sheets in the afternoon! Don't fear, this recipe is the solution to a mess-free, yet totally Mom-worthy breakfast in bed. It's an all-in-one, hands-free breakfast in a challah bowl! *Snuggle up Queen Mom, this is your day!*

Equipment:

Muffin tin, or 6 oz ramekins

Ingredients

24-30 oz challah dough of your choice

Glaze:

1 egg yolk, beaten with 2 tsp water

Filling base:

6 Tbsp melted butter

6 eggs (1 egg per muffin)

Finishing salt and black pepper, to taste

Filling ideas:

1. FETA + CUBED ROASTED SWEET POTATOES + KALE + EGG

2. SHREDDED CHEDDAR + LOX + SPINACH + EGG

3. SHREDDED MOZARELLA + TOMATO + BASIL + EGG

Can you come up with your own combos?

1. Divide the dough into 6 (4-5oz) balls. Round the balls using the rounding method on page 257.

2. Place the rounded balls of challah dough into greased ramekins or muffin tin. Allow to rise for about 30 minutes, until puffy.

3. Preheat the oven to 350°F. Glaze dough with egg. Bake for 25 minutes, until golden and shiny.

4. Allow to cool, then follow instructions on the facing page.

_____ + _____ + _____ + _____

_____ + _____ + _____ + _____

_____ + _____ + _____ + _____

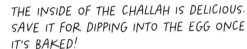

THE INSIDE OF THE CHALLAH IS DELICIOUS. SAVE IT FOR DIPPING INTO THE EGG ONCE IT'S BAKED!

1 Use a knife or spoon to cut out a circle from the top of each challah bun, then scoop some out some of the insides, making sure to leave a good amount of challah.

2 Using a pastry brush, brush the inside with melted butter.

3 See recipe for topping options. Add cheese first, if using.

4 Add vegetables and any greens or herbs. Be sure to leave some room for the egg!

5 Crack an egg into a cup, then carefully pour into each challah hole. Season with salt and pepper. Bake in a 350°F oven for 10-12 minutes, then cover with foil, and bake for another 20 minutes, until eggs are set but still runny. Add a few more minutes for well-done eggs.

★★☆

STUFFED FRENCH TOAST
PB&J or Fluffernutter!

SERVES: 8

Ingredients:

- 4 eggs
- ½ cup milk
- ¼ cup heavy cream
- 1 tsp vanilla extract
- ½ tsp cinnamon
- 1 large challah
- Peanut butter
- Jelly or marshmallow cream
- 1 stick (½ cup) butter or oil, for frying

What's better than French toast? Stuffed French toast!
Oozing with sticky, sweet peanut butter and jelly, or the even more sticky marshmallow cream and peanut butter combo, stuffed French toast is awesome! Each slice is really big, and can easily serve two hungry kids!

1 Whisk the **eggs**, **milk**, **cream**, **vanilla**, and **cinnamon** in a large bowl; set aside.

2 Cut the **challah** into four very thick slices, about 3½-inch thick. Carefully cut into the center of each slice to create a pocket (kind of like a pita), being sure not to go all the way through.

3 Using a spreader or spoon, spread **peanut butter** on one side of the inside of the pocket, and spread either **jelly** or **marshmallow cream** on the other side.

4 Heat 1 tablespoon **butter or oil** in a non-stick skillet over medium heat. Add stuffed challah to the pan, and allow to toast slightly on both sides.

5 Using tongs, carefully transfer the **toasted stuffed challah** to the **egg mixture**, making sure to soak both sides. Heat another **1 tablespoon butter** or **oil** in the skillet, and fry stuffed challah on both sides until golden brown. Repeat with remaining stuffed challah and egg mixture. *Cut diagonally, and enjoy!*

S'MORES FRENCH TOAST

SERVES: 6-8

My favorite thing to watch on airplanes are cooking shows. While sitting on an airplane, on my way to speak at a challah event, the recipe that was being featured was a s'mores sandwich. I was so excited by the idea that I quickly wrote down my thoughts on how to make it even better, and by the time the plane landed, the S'mores French Toast was born!

Ingredients:

 4 eggs

 ¼ cup milk or non-dairy milk

 2 Tbsp sugar

 ½ tsp vanilla extract

 7 whole graham crackers

 ¼ cup (½ stick) butter or margarine, divided

 1 large loaf challah, cut into 8 thick slices

Chocolate hazelnut spread

Mini marshmallows

Topping:

Crushed toasted hazelnuts, optional

1. Whisk the **eggs**, **milk**, **sugar**, and **vanilla** in a large bowl; set aside.

2. Add the **graham crackers** to a large Ziploc bag, then seal and crush with a rolling pin. Alternatively, pulse in a food processor, then transfer crumbs to a deep plate or a shallow bowl — it should be about 1 cup crumbs.

3. Heat 1 Tbsp **butter** in a large non-stick skillet over medium heat.

4. Working two at a time, dip the **challah slices** into the **egg mixture**, and soak on both sides, then dip into the **graham cracker crumbs**.

5. Fry on both sides until golden brown, then transfer to a paper towel-lined plate to absorb excess oil. Repeat with remaining butter, challah, and egg mixture.

6. Spread a generous amount of **chocolate spread** on each slice.

7. Place 4 pieces of French toast on a baking sheet, and top with some **mini marshmallows**. Broil for 1 minute or just until the marshmallows look toasted.

8. Top with remaining pieces of French toast. Serve with **crushed hazelnuts** (if desired) and more marshmallows. Slice in half to get the oozy marshmallow effect!

PUMPKIN FRENCH TOAST

SERVES: 6-8

If by some miracle there is leftover pumpkin challah in your house, you will need to make this recipe. If you don't have pumpkin challah on hand, but the idea of pumpkin French toast on a crisp fall Sunday morning sounds like just the thing you want to eat, then don't worry — read on for a version of this recipe that transforms plain challah into pumpkin French toast.

Ingredients:

- 6 eggs
- 1 cup milk (or non-dairy milk)
- ½ cup heavy cream (or non-dairy creamer)*
- ½ cup brown sugar
- 4 tsp pumpkin pie spice
- 1 tsp cinnamon
- 1 teaspoon salt
- 1 teaspoon vanilla extract
- ¼ cup butter or margarine, divided
- ¼ cup canola or grapeseed oil, divided
- 1 large loaf pumpkin challah, cut into 8 thick slices

Serve with:

Maple syrup

Cinnamon sugar

1. Whisk the **eggs**, **milk**, **heavy cream**, **brown sugar**, **pumpkin pie spice**, **cinnamon**, **salt**, and **vanilla extract** in a large bowl; set aside.

2. Heat **1 tablespoon butter** and **1 tablespoon oil** in a large non-stick skillet over medium heat.

3. Working two at a time, dip the challah slices into the **egg mixture**, and soak on both sides.

4. Fry on both sides until golden brown, then transfer to a paper towel-lined plate to absorb excess oil. Repeat with remaining butter, oil, challah, and egg mixture.

5. Serve with **maple syrup** and **cinnamon sugar**.

NO PUMPKIN CHALLAH? NO PROBLEM!

If you only have regular challah, replace ½ cup cream in the recipe with ½ cup pumpkin purée (not pumpkin pie filling!). Whisk well to incorporate, and proceed with the recipe.

FRUIT ROLL-UPS

YIELD: 16 ROLL-UPS

This is a simple, delicious, and brilliant snack. See what flavor combinations you can come up with yourself!

Ingredients:

18-24 oz of Classic Challah dough (*page 56*) or challah dough of choice

All-purpose flour, for dusting

Confectioners' sugar, optional

Glaze:

1 egg yolk, beaten with 2 tsp water

CINNAPPLE: Thinly sliced apples + melted butter *or* margarine & cinnamon sugar

CHOCO-BANANA: Thinly sliced bananas + chocolate spread

CREAM CHEESE BLUES: Cream Cheese + blueberries

Create your own fun flavor combinations!

Instructions:

1. Roll the **dough** into a large circle.

2. Using a pizza cutter, cut the circle into quarters, then each quarter in half, and then in half again. You should have 16 dough triangles. Dust dough with **flour**.

3. Choose your filling(s). Schmear the **spread** (if using the options above: **margarine** and **cinnamon sugar**; **chocolate spread**; or **cream cheese**) all over each slice, then top with **fruit** or **berries** of choice at the wider end.

4. Roll up from the wider end. Place, seam side down, on a parchment-lined baking sheet, leaving space between each roll-up for rising.

5. Cover loosely with a dish towel, and allow to rise until puffy.

6. **Glaze with egg**, then bake in a 350°F oven for 25 minutes, until golden brown.

7. Allow to cool on a cooling rack, then dust with some **confectioners' sugar** (if desired).

163

ULTIMATE
CHEESE DIPPING
SAUCE

RECIPE ON FOLLOWING SPREAD

PRETZEL CHALLAH BITES

YIELD: 45 PRETZEL BITES

You know that amazing smell that hits you when you walk into a mall? That hot buttery pretzel smell? Now, what if I told you that your house can smell that good?

All you need is some challah dough (the classic works great for this) and a little pretzel bath made from brown sugar and baking soda. This will give you hot, chewy pretzel bites for anytime the munchies hit. You can make this into any shape, and you can even "pretzelize" a classic braided challah. Take one of your challahs this Friday (or all of them!) and give them the royal pretzel treatment. And just like that, you are a challah superhero. *(Cape sold separately.)*

RECIPE & INSTRUCTIONS ON FOLLOWING PAGE

Ingredients:

24 oz Classic Challah dough
(*page 56*)

⅓ cup brown sugar

⅓ cup baking soda

Glaze:

1 egg yolk, beaten with 2 tsp water

Topping:

Pretzel salt

½ cup (1 stick) butter or margarine,
melted

Prep:

Preheat the oven to 350°F
Line a baking sheet with
parchment paper.

WARNING: BOILING WATER INVOLVED.
ADULT SUPERVISON REQUIRED.

*DON'T KEEP THE PRETZEL BITES
IN THE WATER FOR TOO LONG,
OR THEY WILL GET BITTER.*

1 Fill a pot about ¾ full with water, and bring to a boil. Add the **brown sugar**, then carefully add the **baking soda**. *It will bubble over if you dump it all in at once, so pour it in slowly.*

2 Roll the **dough** into a long rope, about 1-inch thick. Using a bench scraper or kitchen scissors, cut the strip into 1-inch pieces.

3 Working in batches of about 15, boil the pieces for about 30 seconds, flipping them halfway through.

4 Using a slotted spoon, transfer to the parchment-lined baking sheet. Make sure the pieces are in a single layer.

5 **Glaze with egg**, then sprinkle with **pretzel salt**. Bake in a 375°F oven for 12-15 minutes, until very dark brown.

6 Brush with **melted butter** while still warm. Optional: Serve with cheese sauce (recipe follows).

★★☆

DAIRY

ULTIMATE CHEESE DIPPING SAUCE

Ingredients:

½ Tbsp butter

½ Tbsp all-purpose flour

½ cup milk

8 oz grated cheddar cheese

1. Melt the **butter** in a saucepan over medium heat. Add the **flour**; whisk continuously for 1 minute.

2. Add the **milk**; keep whisking until incorporated and slightly thickened.

3. Add the **cheddar cheese**; whisk until smooth and melted.

DAIRY *or* PAREVE

GARLIC KNOTS

YIELD: 12-15 GARLIC KNOTS

Even without the Parmesan, these salty, chewy, garlicky knots are going to surprise you with how delicious they are! For a softer, more challah-like garlic knot, use the Classic Challah dough recipe, and for a more chewy, pizza shop-style garlic knot, go with the Water Challah recipe.

Ingredients:

 32oz Classic Challah dough (*page 56*) or Water Challah dough (*page 64*)

 ¼ cup olive oil or melted butter

 ¼ cup chopped garlic*

 1 Tbsp minced fresh parsley (or 2 tsp dried)

 1 Tbsp grated Parmesan, optional

 Coarse sea salt

1. Pour **olive oil** or **butter** into a medium bowl. Add the **chopped garlic**, **parsley**, and **Parmesan** (if desired).

2. Divide **dough** into 12-15 (2-2½ oz) pieces. Roll each piece into a strand, then tie into a knot.

3. Dunk the knotted dough into the **oil-garlic** mixture, rolling it around until completely coated. Place on a parchment-lined baking sheet. Sprinkle with **coarse sea salt** (a little goes a long way!).

4. Allow the knots to rise for 15-25 minutes, then bake in a 410°F oven for about 15 minutes, until golden brown. I dare you to not eat them all — good luck!

 *USE STORE BOUGHT PRE-CHOPPED GARLIC TO MAKE THIS RECIPE SUPER EASY!*

169

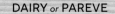

SEUDAH SHLISHIT

Seudat Shlishit, also known in Yiddish-Hebrew as *shalashudis*, is the third meal of Shabbat.

The first meal is Friday night, the second is Shabbat lunch, and the third meal is dinner on Shabbat day before the sun sets. This meal doesn't usually get as much fanfare, especially on short winter Shabbat days when the sun sets before we're even really hungry for dinner.

But in the summer months, when Shabbat stretches way into the evening, *Shalashudis* takes center stage.

After a heavy lunch, we usually like to keep this meal light and fresh. This recipe is perfect.

CHALLAH BRUSCHETTA
TROPICAL OR CLASSIC

YIELD: APPROXIMATELY 10-12 TOASTS

Is it pronounced "broo-shetta" or "broos-ketta?" Even amongst the Italians I asked, there were different opinions. But whatever you call it, everyone will agree that this is a delicious way to eat challah! The traditional Italian bruschetta is toasted sliced bread topped with a fresh tomato salsa. Since we're already creating new traditions with challah bruschetta, why not go exotic with a tropical salsa option as well? This is a great treat for Sunday brunch, but if you toast the challah before Shabbat, you can enjoy it for *Seudat Shlishit* on a long summer Shabbat day.

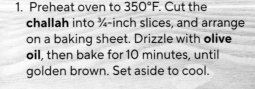

Ingredients:

1 challah

Olive oil

Tropical Sweet Salsa:

1 Tbsp olive oil

½ cup diced mango

½ cup diced avocado

½ cup sliced strawberries

¼ cup finely diced red onion

1 teaspoon minced jalapeño

Juice of 2 limes

Classic Tomato Salsa:

6 plum tomatoes, diced

⅓ cup chopped fresh basil

¼ cup shredded Parmesan cheese

3 cloves garlic, minced

1 Tbsp balsamic vinegar

1 Tbsp olive oil

2 tsp kosher salt

¼ tsp ground black pepper

1. Preheat oven to 350°F. Cut the **challah** into ¾-inch slices, and arrange on a baking sheet. Drizzle with **olive oil**, then bake for 10 minutes, until golden brown. Set aside to cool.

2. For the salsa, mix ingredients together. Chill in the fridge for about 30-60 minutes.

3. Top each piece of toast with **salsa**, (drain out the extra liquid so it doesn't make the toast soggy). Serve immediately.

★★☆

CHALLAH CROUTONS

FOUR WAYS   YIELD: APPROXIMATELY 4 CUPS OF CROUTONS

Sure — you could buy croutons in the store, but once you make these homemade challah croutons, you might never want to eat a store bought version again. As a salad topping, a soup accompaniment, or just a good snack, these croutons are how we keep good challah going, long after Shabbat ends. While you can always use fresh challah to make croutons, using day-old challah (or even challah that's been sitting for a few days!) will give you the best results.

Ingredients:

 1 large loaf day-old challah

GARLICKY GOODNESS

¼ cup melted butter or margarine

2 Tbsp garlic salt (like Lawry's™) or mix garlic, salt and dried parsley

MEDITERRANEAN MUNCHIES

¼ cup olive oil

2 Tbsp za'atar

1 tsp fine sea salt

CINNAMON SWEET

The most addictive snack — hide them so that they don't get eaten in one sitting!

½ cup melted butter or margarine

½ cup sugar

1 Tbsp cinnamon

ITALIAN CLASSIC

This is a classic choice for a Caesar salad.

¼ cup olive oil

2 tsp Italian seasoning

1 tsp garlic powder

1 tsp fine sea salt

1. Preheat oven to 300°F. Cut the crust off the challah, if desired, then cut into cubes. Cut croutons about the same size, to ensure even cooking.

2. Mix the oil (or melted butter) and seasonings of choice. Add the challah cubes and toss until evenly coated.

3. Arrange in a single layer on a parchment-lined baking sheet. Bake for about 30 minutes, tossing carefully halfway through, until lightly golden brown and crispy.

4. Let the croutons cool, then store in a sealed container at room temperature for up to 2 weeks, or freeze for up to 1 month.

PIZZA "CHALLZONE"

YIELD: 8 CHALLZONES

Calzones are the unsung heroes of pizza shops everywhere. They're basically stuffed pizzas that you can hold in your hand. I mean, seriously, does it get any better?

Well, if the dough is a challah dough, and it's stuffed with cheesy heaven and homemade sauce, then yes, it gets better! This is not the calzone, it's the chall-zone (see what I did there?), and it is extremely delicious.

Ingredients:

32-36 oz Water Challah dough (*page 64*)

or Classic Challah dough (*page 56*)

Sauce:

1 (6 oz) jar tomato paste

½ cup favorite pizza sauce

1 Tbsp honey

½ tsp fine sea salt

Filling:

Shredded pizza cheese

Vegetables of choice, such as peppers, olives, mushrooms, and onions

Glaze:

1 egg yolk, beaten with 2 tsp water

Topping:

Grated Parmesan

Fresh chopped parsley

Minced garlic

Melted butter

INSTRUCTIONS ON FOLLOWING PAGE...

175

PIZZA "CHALLZONE"

1 Mix **sauce ingredients** in a medium bowl; set aside.

2 Divide **dough** into 4½-5 oz portions, then roll each ball into an oval shape.

3 Spread the **sauce** into the center of each oval, leaving a bit of a border all around. Top with **shredded cheese**, as well as any **veggies** you like!

4 Using a pizza cutter or bench scraper, make a series of cuts about one-third of the way into the oval on one side. If you want to make it fancier, you can make a bunch of braids or twists with the strands.

5 Roll the uncut dough over the sauce and cheese filling, then wrap the strands around the roll. Bring the 2 ends together to form a circle, and pinch well at the ends to seal.

6 **Glaze with egg**, then sprinkle with **grated Parmesan**, **parsley**, and **minced garlic** (if desired). Bake in a 350°F oven for 25 minutes. Immediately brush with **melted butter** while still warm.

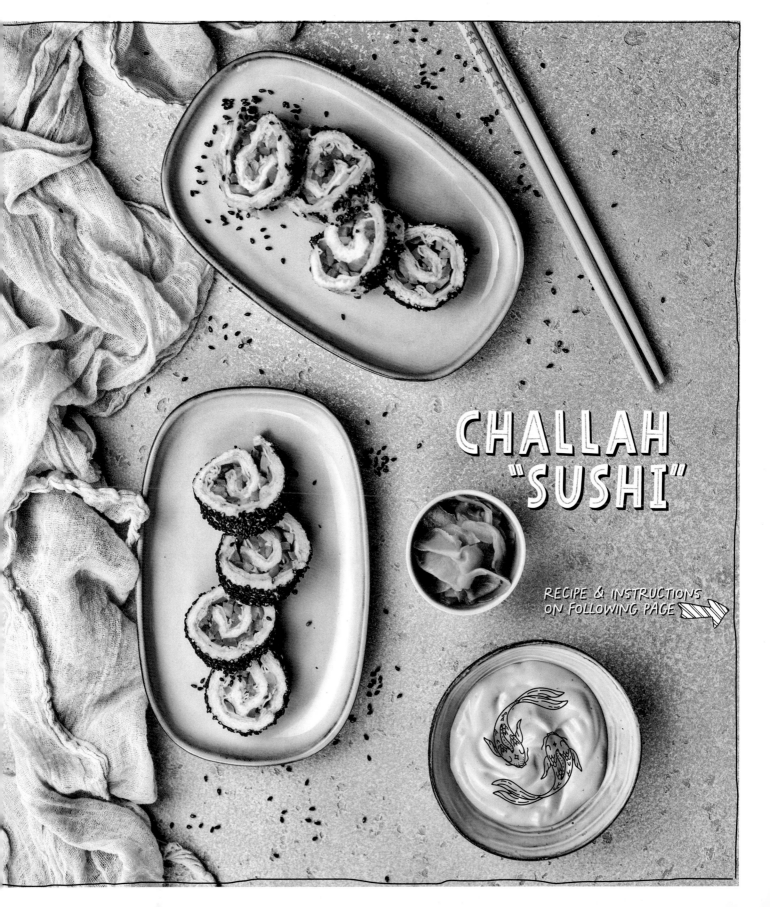

CHALLAH "SUSHI"

RECIPE & INSTRUCTIONS
ON FOLLOWING PAGE

☆☆

CHALLAH "SUSHI"

YIELD: 3 ROLLS OF SUSHI (6-8 PIECES PER ROLL)

This is a super fun take on sushi. The ingredients here are just to spark your own creativity! What's your favorite sandwich? Can you make it work as challah sushi? Pick a base sauce or spread, a protein, and lots of colorful veggies, and see what you can create!

Ingredients:

1 large fresh challah

Sauces, protein, veggies, and greens (see below for ideas)

Black sesame seeds

DAIRY IDEAS:

 Mayonnaise
+
 Sliced cheese
+
 Tomato
+
 Lettuce

PAREVE IDEAS:

 Mayonnaise
+
 Tuna
+
 Celery
+
 Pickles

MEAT IDEAS:

 Honey mustard
+
 Smoked turkey
+
 Cucumber
+
 Red peppers

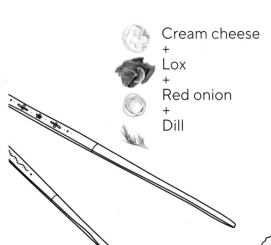

Cream cheese
+
Lox
+
Red onion
+
Dill

 Hummus
+
 Avocado
+
Carrot matchsticks
+
Arugula

 Spicy mayo
+
 Pastrami
+
 Scallions
+
 Purple cabbage

Let's make it!

1 Cut off the crust completely from the **challah**, then slice thinly lengthwise for the largest slices possible.

2 Place a slice of challah between two pieces of plastic wrap. Roll out with a rolling pin until it's thin enough to roll up.

3 Remove the top layer of the plastic wrap. Spread on a layer of a **sauce** of your choice.

4 Add **protein** and **veggies** of your choice.

5 Roll up tightly from the long end using the plastic wrap to hold it together. Squeeze tightly to form a log.

6 Remove plastic wrap. Slice into pieces. Repeat with remaining challah, sauce, and fillings. Optional: Before slicing, brush with some **additional sauce**, then roll in **black sesame seeds** (not pictured) for a fun presentation.

Move over mac and cheese!
We have a new favorite cheesy dish on the menu. If you like spicy food, keep some of the ribs and seeds of the jalapeños in. If not, remove them all, or leave out the jalapeños entirely.

Ingredients:

2 (10 oz) cans Mexicorn*, drained

2 jalapeños, finely diced

1 diced red onion

5 eggs

3 cups milk

1 Tbsp fine sea salt

1 Tbsp chili powder

1 tsp garlic powder

1 tsp black pepper

1 loaf challah, crust cut off, then cut into 1-inch cubes

16 oz shredded sharp cheddar cheese

Salsa, for serving, optional

If Mexicorn (Green Giant™) is not available, just use regular canned corn, and add ½ red bell pepper and ½ green bell pepper, finely diced.

1 Mix the **corn, jalapeños,** and **red onions**. In another bowl, whisk the **eggs, milk,** and **spices**.

2 Place half of the **challah cubes** into a greased 8-inch square or 9x13-inch ovenproof casserole dish. Sprinkle the **corn mixture** over the **challah**, then **half the cheese**. Top with **remaining challah cubes**.

3 Pour the **egg mixture** over the whole dish, pressing down to make sure it's all soaking in the egg mixture.

4 Top with the **remaining cheese**. Allow to rest for 30 minutes or overnight in the fridge. Cover with greased foil, then bake in a 350°F oven for 45-60 minutes.

5 Remove foil and continue to bake, uncovered, for another 20-25 minutes, until cheese is bubbly on top. Allow to rest for a few minutes before serving. Serve with **salsa** on the side.

CHALLAH PANZANELLA

SERVES: 4 ADULTS

Salad in a challah book? What is even happening here? Let's just say, if a salad finds its way into a challah cookbook, you know it has to be good! This makes an amazing light lunch or dinner; if you include the cheese option, it's really a meal in a bowl. I also love this salad for a Sunday brunch; it's a delicious and healthy way to use up the leftover Shabbat challah. Feel free to omit the cheese for a Pareve salad — it will be delicious regardless.

THE CROUTONS:

1 loaf challah, cut into 1-inch cubes

Olive oil, for drizzling

THE SALAD:

6 Persian cucumbers, sliced

1 pint heirloom cherry tomatoes

½ red onion, thinly sliced

THE VINAIGRETTE:

½ cup good quality olive oil

¼ cup balsamic vinegar

1 tsp fine sea salt

½ tsp black pepper

SALAD TOPPINGS:

1 bunch basil leaves, chiffonade (thin strips)

Parmesan shavings, cubes of fresh mozzarella, or crumbled feta cheese, optional

1. Preheat the oven to 275°F. Arrange **challah cubes** in a single layer on a baking sheet. Toss with a bit of **olive oil**. Bake for 20-25 minutes, until slightly golden and dried out, but not too brown. Allow to cool.

2. In a large salad bowl, mix the **cucumbers**, **tomatoes**, and **onions**. Add the **challah cubes** and toss.

3. Shake the **vinaigrette ingredients** well in a jar, then pour over the salad. Toss gently.

4. Add the **basil** (and **cheese**, if desired). Toss again carefully so as not to break up the challah croutons. For best results, let sit for 30 minutes before serving to soak up the flavors.

NOTES:

♥ The challah can be fresh or stale—since you'll be lightly toasting it, it won't make a difference.

♥ The challah croutons can be made in advance and stored in an airtight container or Ziploc bag at room temperature. If you want to make them way in advance, you can freeze them for up to 2 months.

SAUSAGE & SPINACH STRATA

SERVES: 6-8

A strata is a layered casserole dish that typically consists of bread, eggs, and cheese. This is a meat version (without the cheese of course), which is the perfect family-friendly weeknight dinner. The recipe is totally customizable and versatile. I used sausage for the meat and spinach for the green, but you can use any meat (ground beef, hot dogs, salami) and green (kale, collard greens, asparagus) to make it your own!

Equipment:

Food processor

Large non-stick skillet

Oven-to-table casserole dish

Ingredients:

 1 (24 oz) bag chopped frozen spinach, defrosted

 1 Tbsp olive oil

1 onion, diced

4 cloves garlic, minced

 1 (12 oz) package sausages or salami of choice, finely diced or pulsed in food processor

 2 tsp fine sea salt, divided

 1 tsp freshly ground black pepper, divided

 8 eggs

 1½ cups non-dairy milk

 ¼ cup Dijon mustard

 1 large loaf stale challah, cubed (about 7 to 8 cups)

STEP-BY-STEP PHOTOS AND
INSTRUCTIONS ON NEXT PAGE

SAUSAGE AND SPINACH STRATA
Let's make it !

1 Using a tea towel or a few layers of paper towels, squeeze out any extra liquid from the **spinach**; set aside.

Heat **olive oil** in a non-stick skillet over medium-high heat. Add the **onions** and **garlic**, and sauté until softened. Add the **sausages** or **salami**; sauté until golden brown, about 5 minutes.

3 Add the **spinach**, and season with 1 tsp **salt** and ½ tsp **pepper**.

4 Whisk the **eggs**, **non-dairy milk**, **Dijon**, and **remaining salt** and **pepper**.

Arrange half the **challah cubes** in a casserole dish.
Scatter half the **sausage-spinach mixture** over the challah cubes, then pour half the **egg mixture** all over.

Repeat with remaining **challah**, **sausage mixture**, and **egg mixture**. Cover with foil, and refrigerate for 2-3 hours or overnight. Bring the strata to room temperature for about 30 minutes, then bake uncovered in a 350°F oven for 1 hour. Allow to stand for 10 minutes before serving.

SALAMI CHALLAH STUFFING

RECIPE & INSTRUCTIONS ON FOLLOWING PAGE

SALAMI CHALLAH STUFFING

SERVES: 6-8

Stuffings made with challah are the best, and this one is the best of the best! Use this the traditional way, to stuff a turkey or chicken, or serve it as a side dish, and watch all the main dishes get ignored! Although very similar, what sets a stuffing apart from a strata (like the one on the previous page) is that the "custard" of the stuffing typically uses only eggs and broth, whereas the strata is creamier and includes some kind of milk in the custard. If you have any challah leftover after Shabbat, just dice it up into cubes, and freeze it in a Ziploc bag — it will be ready for this recipe whenever you are!

Equipment:

Food processor

Large non-stick skillet

Oven-to-table casserole dish

Ingredients:

1 large loaf challah, cubed

1 large sweet onion, chopped

2 large carrots, chopped

4 stalks celery, chopped

10 button or cremini mushrooms, halved

2 Tbsp olive oil

1 (16 oz) salami, diced

¼ cup chopped fresh parsley

2 tsp chopped fresh sage

1 Tbsp poultry seasoning
(such as McCormick™ seasoned salt)

1-2 tsp fine sea salt*

½-1 tsp freshly ground black pepper

4 eggs, lightly beaten

1 cup low-sodium* vegetable or chicken broth, plus more if needed

¾-1 cup orange juice

*If not using low-sodium stock, leave out the salt.
  Remember — the salami has a lot of salt as well!

1 Preheat the oven to 325°F. Arrange the **challah cubes** in a single layer on 2 parchment-lined baking sheets. Bake for 10-15 minutes, until golden and toasted. Allow to cool.

2 Place the **chopped onions**, **carrots**, **celery**, and **mushrooms** into a food processor fitted with the S-blade attachment; pulse just until roughly chopped.

3

Heat the **olive oil** in a large non-stick skillet over medium-high heat. Add the **vegetable mixture**, and sauté until vegetables are slightly caramelized, about 15 minutes.

4

Add the **salami** and **chopped herbs**, and sauté until the salami is browned and crisp. Add the **poultry seasoning**, **salt***, and **pepper**. Sauté for another minute.

5

Transfer the **vegetable mixture** to a large bowl with the **toasted challah cubes**; toss until well combined.

6

Whisk the **eggs**, **broth**, and **orange juice** in a medium bowl.

7

Slowly pour the **egg mixture** over the **challah mixture**; toss to coat, adding **more broth** or **orange juice** if the mixture looks dry. Allow to stand and soak for 10 minutes.

8

Transfer the mixture to a greased casserole dish, and cover tightly with foil. Bake for 45 minutes, then uncover and bake until golden, about 15 more minutes. Allow to stand for 10 minutes before serving.

★★☆

HOT DIGGITY DOG CHALLAH

MEAT

FEEDS A HUNGRY CROWD!

Hot diggity dog!
This is the challah version of franks 'n blanks! If you have some challah dough, about 18-24 oz, to spare (about the amount of one medium/large challah), use it to make this delicacy as a pre-Shabbat snack for all the hungry people that wander into the kitchen! This is also a fun idea for a party. Everyone can just pull off a challah-covered dog, and dunk it in whatever sauce you choose.

Ingredients:

24 oz Classic Challah dough
(*page 56*)

All-purpose flour, for dusting

12 hot dogs

Glaze:

1 egg yolk, beaten with 2 tsp water

Mustard or ketchup, for serving

Preheat the oven to 350°F. Divide dough into 2 equal portions. Roll each portion into a large circle. Place on a silicone baking mat or parchment-lined baking sheet. Sprinkle flour over the first dough circle, then top with the second dough circle.

Place a small oven-proof bowl or ramekin in the center, pressing down to make a hole. Remove that center piece of dough, then place the bowl back in the hole.

Working around the bowl, use a pizza cutter or bench scraper to cut 16 slits through both dough circles around the bowl.

Cut each hot dog into 3 pieces. Place a hot dog piece on each top strip of dough, then roll up. Repeat with the bottom strips of dough, tucking each rolled up piece under the top pieces. Glaze with egg, then bake for 25-30 minutes.

THE SWEET CHALLAH LIFE

CHALLAH
FOR DESSERT

CHOCOLATE-HAZELNUT TWISTS

YIELD: 24 TWISTS

A simple recipe that you're going to turn to again and again. This is a great use for some extra challah dough. It's also super quick and easy, and looks so pretty.

Ingredients:

32 oz Classic Challah dough
(*page 56*)

1 cup hazelnut chocolate spread

1 cup finely chopped hazelnuts

Glaze:

1 egg, beaten with 2 tsp water

Confectioners' sugar,
for sprinkling

1 Roll the **dough** into a large rectangle. Spread **hazelnut spread** in a thin, even layer on the dough, leaving a ¼-inch border around the edges. Sprinkle the **chopped hazelnuts** over the filling.

2 Fold one-third of the dough over the filling, then fold the exposed third on top of that.

3 Using a rolling pin, roll the dough into one long rectangle.

4 Using a pizza cutter or bench scraper, cut the dough into 1½-inch strips. Working one at a time, twist each strip, then roll it up into a knot.

5 Place on parchment lined baking sheet. Cover and allow to rise for about 30 minutes or until puffy. **Glaze with egg**, and then bake at 350° F for 12-15 minutes.

6 Allow the twists to cool slightly before sprinkling with **confectioners' sugar**.

FUDGY CHOCOLATE-CHIP DESSERT PIZZA

RECIPE & INSTRUCTIONS ON FOLLOWING PAGE

FUDGY CHOCOLATE-CHIP DESSERT PIZZA

Dessert pizzas are always an excellent idea. They became a bit of a craze in the upscale kosher pizza shops in Brooklyn, and for good reason. If you have a little bit of extra challah dough on hand, you can make this incredible dessert that looks like it came straight out of a Brooklyn café. Use the chocolate chip cookie filling recipe below, or for a shortcut, use a boxed chocolate chip cookie mix, like Duncan Hines™. Either way, this recipe is always a big hit!

Equipment

12-inch pizza pan

Chocolate Chip Cookie Filling:

 2 cups all-purpose flour

1½ tsp cornstarch

1 tsp baking soda

½ tsp fine sea salt

¾ cup canola oil

1 cup packed brown sugar

¼ cup sugar

1 large egg + 1 large egg yolk, at room temperature

2 tsp vanilla extract

1 cup chocolate chips

Pizza crust:

1-2 lb challah dough

Topping:

8 oz heavy cream (or 1 can coconut cream), whipped with ¾ cup confectioners' sugar

Fresh fruit and berries

1 Preheat oven to 350°F. Mix the **flour**, **cornstarch**, **baking soda**, and **salt** in a medium bowl; set aside.

2 In a large bowl, whisk the **oil** and **sugars** until smooth, then whisk in the **eggs** and **vanilla extract**.

3 Pour the dry ingredients mixture into the wet ingredients and mix together until well combined. Add the **chocolate chips** and mix to incorporate.

4 Roll dough into a 13-inch circle. Spray a 12-inch pizza pan with non-stick spray, then stretch the dough onto it, rolling the edges for a crust. This will ensure that the filling won't leak out during baking. Press the chocolate chip cookie dough evenly onto the challah dough.

5 Bake for 20 minutes, until the crust is a nice golden color. Carefully transfer pizza to a wire cooling rack. Allow to cool completely. Top with **whipped cream** and **fruit** of choice.

RECIPE & INSTRUCTIONS ON FOLLOWING PAGE

PINK
SNOWFLAKE
CHALLAH

PINK SNOWFLAKE CHALLAH

It's snowing pink! This gorgeous challah/babka resembles a magical pink snowflake, and is so much fun to make (and eat)!

Equipment:

Large bowl with sharp edge

Small bowl or round cookie cutter

Ingredients:

 2 lb Brioche (*page 68*)
or any sweet challah dough

Confectioners' sugar, for sprinkling

Berry Cheese Filling:

 1 (8 oz) package cream cheese, brick style, at room temperature

 4 cups confectioners' sugar

 1 egg yolk

1 tsp vanilla extract

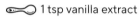 ½ cup raspberry or strawberry jam

1 Add all ingredients for the berry cheese filling to a bowl, and mix with a hand mixer (or stand mixer) until smooth. Set aside.

2 Divide the dough into 4 (8 oz) portions. Roll each of the portions into a circle, a little bigger than the rim of a large bowl.

6 Using a small bowl, ramekin, or cookie cutter, mark the center of the circle, pressing down just to make a mark, but not cutting into the dough. You can keep it in place while making the snowflake.

7 Cut the dough into 4 equal sections, then divide each of those in half, and each of those in half as well, for a total of 16 sections. (Like slicing a pizza pie!)

GREAT JOB FOR LITTLEST HANDS!

3 Transfer **one circle** to a parchment-lined baking sheet. Spread a thin, even layer of **berry cheese filling** on the surface of the **dough**.

4 Top with a **second dough circle**, then spread a thin, even layer of **filling** on the surface. Top with a **third dough circle**, then spread another thin, even layer of **filling** on the surface. Finally, top with the **fourth dough circle**.

5 Place a large bowl upside down over the dough, pressing down hard to cut it into a perfect circle. Remove the bowl, and discard the edge pieces.

8 Grab hold of 2 neighboring sections, twist them 3 times in opposite directions, then pinch together at the top. Repeat with all 16 sections of dough; you will end up with an 8-pointed snowflake shape.

9 Bake in a 350°F oven for 25 minutes, until the top is lightly golden brown. Dust all over with **confectioners' sugar** to get a beautiful snowy effect.

CINNAMON SNAIL ROLLS
with CREAM CHEESE FROSTING

Ingredients:

½ cup sugar

2 tsp cinnamon

16-18 oz Classic Challah dough (*page 56*) or any sweet dough of your choice

½ stick melted butter or margarine

Cream Cheese Frosting:

4 oz cream cheese*, softened at room temperature

4 Tbsp (½ stick) unsalted butter or margarine, softened at room temperature

1 cup confectioners' sugar

1 tsp vanilla extract

Pinch of fine sea salt salt

¼ cup milk*, plus more as needed

Toppings:

Mini marshmallows

Mini chocolate chips

*To make a pareve cream cheese frosting, use a non-dairy cream cheese like Tofutti™ or Wayfair brand™, and a non-dairy milk.

Challah creatures are so much fun! This is a great project to do with even the littlest chefs. From dipping the strands into the cinnamon-sugar mixture to decorating with little marshmallow toothpick eyes — this is a super fun activity that ends up being a yummy treat.

LOTS OF FUN FOR LITTLE HANDS

1 Mix **sugar** and **cinnamon** on a plate; set aside.
Divide the **dough** into 6 (3-ounce) portions. Roll each portion into a skinny log.

2 Dip each log into **melted butter**, then into the prepared **cinnamon-sugar** mixture. Place onto a parchment-lined baking sheet.

3 Roll up like a snail, leaving the ends loose for the "head," and pinching the bottoms for a "tail." Bake in a 350°F oven for 25 minutes. Allow to cool.

4 Whisk **cream cheese** and **butter**. Add **confectioners' sugar, vanilla**, and **salt**; whisk well to combine. Add **milk**, 1 tablespoon at a time, whisking until the mixture is a pourable consistency.

5 Once the challahs are cool, stick **mini marshmallows** onto the top of toothpicks, and insert two into the "head" of each snail. Press **mini chocolate chips** onto the marshmallows for the eyes. Alternatively, "glue" the chocolate chips on with a tiny bit of frosting. Decorate with cream cheese frosting (photo 6).

RECIPE & INSTRUCTIONS ON FOLLOWING PAGE

CHOCOLATE-ORANGE
BABKA WREATH

★★★

CHOCOLATE-ORANGE BABKA WREATH

There's a babka recipe in my first cookbook, *Rising*. It's a good recipe, very good in fact! But I've tasted a lot of babka between then and now, and I think this one is even better. The addition of the orange makes the flavor profile so much more interesting, but you can choose to leave it out if orange isn't your thing, and it is still an incredible filling for a babka. The filling recipe is adapted from my sister-in-law Chani's recipe. She's a master baker, and her babka is legendary. Also, her daughter is one of my lovely nieces pictured making this babka recipe. *How perfect is that?*

Equipment:

Hand or stand mixer

Ingredients:

 32 oz Classic Challah dough (*page 56*) or Brioche dough (*page 68*)

Filling:

♡♡ 2 eggs

¾ cup confectioners' sugar

1¼ cups chocolate chips

1½ sticks margarine or butter

Zest of 1 orange

1 tsp vanilla extract

1 tsp orange extract or 2 tsp orange liqueur, such as Cointreau

1 tsp cinnamon

Orange Glaze:

⅓ cup water

⅓ cup sugar

1 tsp orange extract (or orange liqueur, such as Cointreau)

Thinly sliced orange peel, for garnish

1 Using a hand mixer, beat the **eggs** and **confectioners' sugar** until nice and creamy.

> IF MAKING THE DOUGH ESPECIALLY FOR THIS RECIPE, GO AHEAD AND ADD SOME ORANGE ZEST INTO THE DOUGH ITSELF.

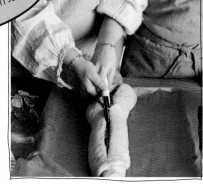

5 Once cool, slice the dough in half lengthwise, leaving a bit attached at the top.

2 Add the **chocolate chips** and **margarine** to a microwave-safe bowl, and microwave in 30-second intervals until melted. Add the **melted chocolate** to the **egg and sugar mixture**.

3 Add the **orange zest**, **vanilla**, **orange extract**, and **cinnamon**. Mix well until mixture thickens.

4 Roll **dough** into a large rectangle. Spread **chocolate mixture** in a thin, even layer on the dough. Roll up, jelly roll-style, and freeze for 10-15 minutes.

6 Twist the two halves together, bringing it all together into a circular wreath shape. Place on a parchment-lined baking sheet or in an 8-inch round pan. Bake in a 350°F oven for 30-35 minutes.

7 While babka is baking, add **glaze ingredients** to a small saucepan over high heat. Bring to a boil, then simmer on low heat for 3 minutes.

8 When the babka is finished baking, immediately drizzle on the **glaze**. Garnish with **orange peel**.

WHITE-CHOCOLATE HAZELNUT RAINBOW BABKA

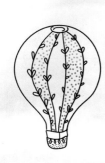

RECIPE & INSTRUCTIONS ON FOLLOWING PAGE

★★☆ DAIRY *or* PAREVE

WHITE-CHOCOLATE HAZELNUT RAINBOW BABKA

YIELD: 2 RAINBOW BABKAS

Rainbow challahs are awesome. But you know what's even better? Rainbow BABKA.
The flavor in this babka is a combination of white chocolate and hazelnut, which is the perfect base for the food coloring of your choice (see page 252 for suggestions on more natural alternatives). You can make the filling yourself at home using this recipe, or buy a store-bought white chocolate hazelnut spread instead.

Dough:

2 lb Classic Challah dough (*page 56*)
or Brioche dough (*page 64*)

Filling:*

7 oz white chocolate, roughly chopped

4 cups (20 oz) roasted unsalted hazelnuts

½ tsp fine sea salt

1 Tbsp canola oil

1 Tbsp vanilla extract

Food coloring of choice

Confectioners' sugar, for sprinkling

Make the filling:

1. Melt the Chocolate: Add the **white chocolate** to a microwave-safe bowl. Microwave in 30-second increments, stirring in between, until melted.

2. Add **hazelnuts** and **salt** to a blender or food processor fitted with the S-blade attachment. (*see photo 1*) Process or blend on a low setting for about 1 minute. Once coarsely crumbled, use a rubber or silicone spatula to scrape down the side. Process again on high for about 1 minute, then scrape down the sides again.

3. Add the **melted white chocolate**, **oil**, and **vanilla extract**. Process again on high until creamy. (*see photo 2*)

4. Divide **white chocolate hazelnut spread** into separate bowls, and mix with **food colorings** of choice.

5. If not making the babka right away, store the spread in an airtight container in the fridge. It will stay fresh for up to 3 weeks.

6. See the opposite page for instructions on assembling the babka!

* *There is a kosher white chocolate spread available on the market! If you want to take a shortcut, you can use that spread and just add food coloring.*

> DID YOU KNOW?
> RAINBOWS ARE IN THE TORAH! THE VERY FIRST RAINBOW WAS A SIGN OF HASHEM'S PROMISE TO NOACH AFTER THE WORLD WAS FLOODED, THAT THE WORLD WILL NEVER AGAIN BE DESTROYED, AND THAT HASHEM WILL ALWAYS PROTECT US.

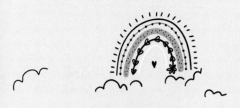

MAKE THE FILLING:

ASSEMBLE THE BABKA:

Roll out the **dough** into a large rectangle. Using an offset spatula or the back of a spoon, spread the **colored white chocolate spread** in stripes like a rainbow! Be sure to wipe down the spatula between colors.

Roll up the dough jelly roll-style. Place on a baking sheet and freeze for about 10 minutes to firm up.

3 Using a pizza cutter or a bench scraper, cut the dough in half lengthwise, leaving a bit attached at the top.

Twist the 2 halves together. Place in a parchment-lined loaf pan. Bake in a 350°F oven for 30 minutes, until golden on top. Sprinkle with **confectioners' sugar** before serving.

PECAN PIE BABKA BUNS

LOTS TO DO FOR THE LITTLEST HANDS

YIELD: 12 BABKA BUNS

A babka bun like no other! Filled with the ooey gooey goodness of pecan pie, and wrapped in delicious challah dough. Don't be intimidated by the fact that this has an extra cooking step; it's super easy and comes together very quickly. Enjoy!

Equipment:

Saucepan

8- or 10-inch round pan, or 9x13-inch pan

Ingredients:

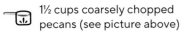 1½ cups coarsely chopped pecans (see picture above)

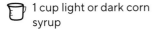 1 cup light or dark corn syrup

 1 cup sugar

 3 eggs

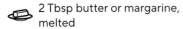 2 Tbsp butter or margarine, melted

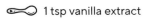 1 tsp vanilla extract

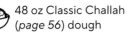 48 oz Classic Challah (*page 56*) dough

Glaze:

1 egg, beaten with 2 tsp water

Cream Cheese Frosting:
(*page 204*)

or Vanilla Glaze:
(*page 229*)

CHOP THE PECANS

1

Heat **pecans**, **corn syrup**, **sugar**, **eggs**, **butter**, and **vanilla** in a saucepan over low heat. Whisk to combine, then stir occasionally until it thickens and reaches a spreadable consistency. Set aside to cool.

3 Roll up dough jelly roll-style.

2

Roll the **dough** into a large rectangle. Spread filling in an even layer over the dough.

4

Cut 2-inch pieces, then arrange in a pan of choice, leaving some room in between each bun for rising. **Glaze with egg**. Cover the pan, and allow it to rise for 30-40 minutes. Bake in a 350°F oven for 30 minutes. Allow to cool, then drizzle with **cream cheese frosting** or **icing glaze**.

DRUNKEN MONKEY CHALLAH

Is it made with challah dough? YES.
Is it cake? YES.

Monkey bread, essentially a cake made out of tiny pieces of dough dipped in cinnamon and sugar, has been around for a long time. I have always loved the name because I think monkeys are funny, but when I thought of making this recipe with challah and adding some rum, I realized I can call it a drunken monkey challah, and I think we can all agree that drunk monkeys are the funniest.

This challah/cake/monkey concoction is drippy, oozing with sticky caramel and rum (or rum extract if your parents don't want you getting into their liquor cabinet just yet!), and has got to be one of the best things that you can do with your challah dough.

Also, it's super fun to make, and even more fun to say. Let's make it together!

RECIPE & INSTRUCTIONS ON FOLLOWING PAGE

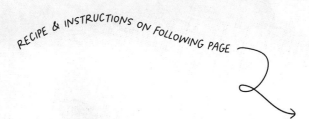

217

★★☆

DRUNKEN MONKEY CHALLAH

YIELD: 1 DRUNK MONKEY CAKE

Equipment:

Saucepan

Bundt or tube pan (*if using a tube pan, make sure it's not the kind with a removable bottom, as the sauce will leak out!*)

Ingredients:

1 cup pecans

24-28 oz Classic Challah dough (*page 56*), or other sweet challah dough (such as Maple Challah (*page 86*), Pumpkin Challah (*page 74*), or Gingerbread Challah (*page 80*)

1 cup of brown sugar

2 tsp of ground cinnamon

Drunken Monkey Sauce:

½ cup (1 stick) butter or margarine

⅔ cup brown sugar

⅓ cup maple syrup

2 Tbsp rum or bourbon (or 2 tsp rum extract)

Add ¾ cup **pecans** to a Ziploc bag, then crush using a rolling pin or meat mallet.

Grease a Bundt or tube pan very well. Place **¼ cup pecans** at the bottom of the pan — this will end up as the top of the monkey bread! Preheat oven to 350°F.

Cut the **dough** into 1½-inch pieces. You should end up with 60-75 pieces.

Working in batches of about 15, **wet your hands** and lightly tap the pieces of dough so that they get slightly sticky.

Add **brown sugar** and **cinnamon** to a Ziploc bag; shake to mix. Working one at a time, add a piece of dough to the bag, and shake to coat before adding the next one. Repeat until all 15 pieces of the first batch are coated in the bag.

Transfer **coated dough pieces** to the pan. Sprinkle with **chopped pecans**. Repeat with remaining pieces of dough, working in batches of 15 — wet, shake, layer, sprinkle **pecans**, and repeat. Be sure to layer the dough pieces randomly over each other. (Pretend you're an actual drunk monkey — don't be exact!)

Now let's make the sauce! Add **butter**, **brown sugar**, **maple syrup**, and **rum** to a saucepan over high heat. Bring to a boil, then lower heat and simmer for about 1-2 minutes, stirring constantly. Watch it carefully so the sugar doesn't harden. Carefully pour the **hot sauce** over the dough.

Cover with a dish towel, and allow to rise for about 15 minutes, then bake in a 350°F oven for 20-25 minutes. Place a piece of foil or baking sheet underneath the pan in the oven to catch any sauce that might spill while baking. Allow monkey bread to cool for 10 minutes. Carefully invert monkey bread onto a cake plate, then start pulling off pieces of pure yumminess!

SERVE CHALLAH KUGEL WARM
& POUR ON LOTS OF THE
VANILLA ANGLAISE SAUCE!

Plan ahead!
THIS RECIPE WORKS REALLY WELL IF
REFRIGERATED OVERNIGHT BEFORE BAKING.
SIMPLY PREPARE IT RIGHT AFTER SHABBAT
WITH ANY LEFTOVER BITS OF CHALLAH,
AND ENJOY A DECADENT BRUNCH DESSERT
ON SUNDAY!

WHITE CHOCOLATE CHALLAH KUGEL

This is not your average challah kugel.

Kugel, similar to an English pudding, is really just another name for a cake — savory or sweet — made from a starch like noodle, bread, or potatoes, and mixed with eggs and other good stuff, then baked until golden and delicious.

In this version, chunks of white chocolate are tucked into fluffy challah pillows that are then soaked in a bath of vanilla and cream. Try not to eat it straight from the oven with the crispy bits of challah and oozy chocolate — wait for the hot vanilla anglaise to be poured all over it. This is truly a challah dessert at its best.

RECIPE & INSTRUCTIONS
ON FOLLOWING PAGE

WHITE CHOCOLATE CHALLAH KUGEL

YIELD: 1 LARGE OR 8 INDIVIDUAL

Ingredients:

 1 large loaf challah

 1½ bars white chocolate, roughly chopped

 3 cups whole milk (or full-fat coconut milk)

 1 cup heavy cream (or non-dairy whipping cream)

 5 eggs

 1¾ cups sugar

 1 Tbsp vanilla extract

½ tsp cinnamon

Vanilla Anglaise Sauce:

 1 cup heavy cream

 1 Tbsp vanilla extract

 4 egg yolks

 ½ cup vanilla sugar

¼ tsp cinnamon

1 Cut the **challah** into 1-inch cubes and roughly chop the **white chocolate**.

2 Grease a 9x13-inch baking dish or 8 ramekins. Add **challah** and **white chocolate**, evenly interspersing the chocolate throughout.

222

3 Whisk the **milk**, **cream**, **eggs**, **sugar**, **vanilla**, and **cinnamon** in a large mixing bowl.

4 Pour the **egg mixture** over the **chopped challah** and **chocolate**, using only as much of the egg mixture as needed to soak the challah, but not too much that the custard pools around the challah. Let challah soak for at least 30 minutes, or refrigerate, covered, overnight. Bake, uncovered, in a 350°F oven for 35-40 minutes. Serve warm with vanilla anglaise sauce.

MAKE THE SAUCE!

Add **cream** and **vanilla** in a saucepan over medium heat. Cook until bubbles begin to form along the edges.

Whisk **egg yolks**, **vanilla sugar** and **cinnamon** in a bowl.

3 Temper the **egg mixture** by adding **one tablespoon of the hot cream** into the egg mixture and whisking quickly. Then, pour the remaining egg mixture into the saucepan while whisking quickly. Continue cooking until the sauce thickens and coats the back of a spoon.

TEMPERING EGGS:

Tempering eggs means bringing them to a hot temperature slowly, otherwise the eggs will start cooking when you put them in the hot liquid. *Yuck! Nobody wants scrambled eggs in their dessert!*

Here's the technique:

1. Add one tablespoon of the hot cream into the egg mixture to warm up the eggs a little. Whisk it quickly.

2. Add another spoon of the hot cream into the eggs and whisk it quickly again. Keep adding in small amounts of the hot liquid until the eggs are nice and warmed up, then you can pour the whole egg mixture into the hot cream and whisk quickly one last time.

223

CINNAMON-STREUSEL CRUNCH PUDDING *

Every time a recipe calls for a crunchy topping, I automatically double the topping. I'm a firm believer in a 2:1 crunch ratio! Of course, if I'm the one actually writing the recipe, you know there will be plenty of crunch!

This recipe is going to provide you with all the crunchy satisfaction you desire —creamy on the bottom, crunchy on the top, hot and oozing cinnamony goodness. Topped with a scoop of ice cream, of course!

Enjoy!

RECIPE & INSTRUCTIONS ON FOLLOWING PAGE

* Not a pudding in the American sense. a pudding as in the British sense, which is really a challah kugel or cake. See note on previous recipe for more details!

★★☆

DAIRY *or* PAREVE

CINNAMON-STREUSEL CRUNCH PUDDING*

SERVES: 12-15

Equipment:

Pastry Cutter

Oven-to-table 9x13-inch casserole dish

Ingredients:

- 1 large loaf challah
- 2 cups whole milk or full-fat coconut milk
- 2 cup heavy cream or non-dairy substitute
- 2 cups sugar
- 8 whole eggs
- 2 Tbsp cinnamon
- 1 Tbsp vanilla extract

Topping:

- 4 Tbsp butter (½ stick), softened
- 1 cup firmly packed brown sugar
- ½ cup chopped walnuts or pecans, optional
- ⅓ cup flour
- 2 tsp cinnamon

Ice cream or whipped cream, for serving

226

1 Cut the **challah** into 1-inch cubes; place in a large mixing bowl.

2 Whisk the **milk, cream, sugar, eggs, cinnamon**, and **vanilla** in a medium mixing bowl.

3 Pour the **milk mixture** over the challah; let challah soak for at least 30 minutes or cover and refrigerate overnight.

4 While the challah is soaking, let's make the streusel. Mix the topping ingredients in a medium bowl, using your fingers or a pastry cutter, until the consistency is like wet sand.

5 Preheat the oven to 325°F. Grease a 9x13-inch baking dish with baking spray or butter. Pour in the soaked challah, draining out any of the excess custard.

6 Add the **streusel** over the challah in an even layer. Bake, uncovered, for 50-60 minutes, until the center is firm and set. Serve warm with ice cream or whipped cream.

227

TOP IT, DIP IT, STUFF IT OR SPREAD IT

CHALLAH
TOPPINGS & FILLINGS

ICING GLAZES

The Method:

1. Mix all the ingredients together except for the milk.

2. Add the milk slowly, mixing continuously, until the mixture is very smooth and just pourable.

3. If not using immediately, store in an airtight container in the fridge. If needed, add a drop of liquid to loosen the glaze once ready to use.

LEMON GLAZE

1½ cups confectioners' sugar

1 tsp lemon extract

2-3 Tbsp milk of choice (dairy or non-dairy)

Yellow food coloring, optional
(this will make it look more "lemony")

VANILLA GLAZE

1½ cups confectioners' sugar

1 tsp vanilla extract

2-3 Tbsp milk of choice (dairy or non-dairy)

Food coloring, optional

PEANUT BUTTER GLAZE

1½ cups confectioners' sugar

1 Tbsp creamy peanut butter

3-5 Tbsp milk of choice (dairy or non-dairy)

SWEET & CRUNCHY TOPPINGS

YIELD: 1 ½ - 2 CUPS, ENOUGH TO TOP 4 CHALLAHS

The Method:

1. If any of the biscuits or cookies need to be crushed into crumbs, either place into a Ziploc bag and, using a meat mallet or rolling pin, bang until crumbly, or place into a food processor fitted with the S-blade, and pulse just until broken up and a slightly crumbly.

2. Mix all the ingredients together in a bowl except for the butter.

3. Make sure butter or margarine is cold; cut into cubes.

4. Using a pastry cutter or your fingers, mix the butter into the dry mixture to create a crumbly texture. Keep mixing until the butter is all incorporated and there are no big chunks remaining. The mixture should resemble wet sand.

Note: All crunchy toppings can be stored in an airtight container in the fridge for up to a month.

BASIC CRUMB STREUSEL

½ cup sugar

½ cup all-purpose flour

2 tsp cinnamon, optional

4 Tbsp (½ stick) unsalted butter or margarine

LEMON SHORTBREAD STREUSEL

1 cup all-purpose flour

⅓ cup vanilla sugar

1 Tbsp lemon zest

¼ tsp fine sea salt

½ cup (1 stick) unsalted butter or margarine

GRAHAM CRACKERS SMORES CRUNCH

9 graham crackers, crushed (see Method, step #1)

½ tsp cinnamon

4 Tbsp (½ stick) unsalted butter or margarine

¼ cup mini chocolate chips

¼ cup mini marshmallows

LOTUS™ CRUMBLE

20 speculoos cookies, such as Lotus™, crushed
(see Method, step #1)

⅓ cup all-purpose flour

½ tsp fine sea salt

1 tsp ground ginger

4 Tbsp (½ stick) unsalted butter

HALVAH PISTACHIO CRUMBLE

⅔ cup crushed unsalted pistachios
(if using salted, then skip the pinch of salt)

½ cup all-purpose flour

½ cup crumbled halva

¼ cup sugar

¼ cup lightly packed light brown sugar

½ tsp fine sea salt

3 Tbsp unsalted butter or margarine

BIRTHDAY CAKE CRUNCH

24 vanilla sandwich cookies, crushed
(see Method, step #1)

½ cup non-pareils sprinkles

Vanilla Icing Glaze (see recipe on previous spread)

MAPLE PECAN OAT CRUNCH

½ cup packed dark brown sugar

½ cup all-purpose flour

¼ cup old-fashioned rolled oats

¼ cup roughly chopped pecans

1 tsp cinnamon

1 tsp maple extract

6 Tbsp unsalted butter or margarine

SALTY, MUNCHY TOPPINGS

For the recipes that use butter, see 'The Method' in the previous spread, "Sweet and Crunchy Toppings."

DUKKAH CRUNCH

½ cup hazelnuts, chopped

¼ cup coriander seeds

3 Tbsp sesame seeds

2 Tbsp cumin seeds, crushed

1 Tbsp black peppercorns, crushed

1 tsp fennel seeds, crushed

1 tsp dried mint

1 tsp fine sea salt

4 Tbsp (½ stick) butter or margarine, chilled and cut into cubes

SAVORY OAT CRUNCH

1 cup old-fashioned oats

2 Tbsp slivered almonds

2 Tbsp sunflower seeds

2 Tbsp pumpkin seeds

2 Tbsp sesame seeds

2 tsp maple syrup

1 tsp flax seeds

1 tsp fine sea salt

¼ tsp chili powder, optional

4 Tbsp (½ stick) butter or margarine, chilled and cut into cubes

EVERYTHING SPICE MIX

Mix equal amounts of:

Dehydrated onion flakes

Poppy seeds

Sesame seeds

Dried minced garlic

Coarse salt, to taste

CRUNCHY FRENCH FRIED ONIONS*

5 large onions, thinly sliced

2 cups non-dairy buttermilk*

3 cups all-purpose flour

2 tsp fine sea salt

½ tsp freshly ground black pepper

4 cups canola or grapeseed oil, for frying

1. Soak the **sliced onions** in the **buttermilk**; set aside. Prepare a wire cooling rack set on top of a baking sheet.

2. Mix **flour**, **salt**, and **pepper** in a large bowl.

3. Heat a few inches of **oil** In a large, deep frying pan until it shimmers. To test the oil if it's ready for frying, dip the handle of a wooden spoon into the oil; if it bubbles around the handle, then it's ready.

4. Transfer the **buttermilk-soaked onions** to the **flour mixture**, shaking off as much excess liquid as possible. Toss the onions in the flour until coated.

5. Working in batches, being careful not to overcrowd the pan, fry **onions** until golden brown. Using a slotted spoon, transfer to the prepared rack to drain Use immediately for best results, or store in an airtight container in the fridge for a few days.

*Pour 2 tablespoons lemon juice or white vinegar into a 2-cup glass measuring cup.
  Fill with soy milk or almond milk to make 2 cups; set aside for a few minutes until milk begins to curdle.

HOT & SPICY CRUNCH

1½ cup BBQ corn chips, crushed

¼ cup all-purpose flour

1 Tbsp hot sauce, or to taste

4 Tbsp (½ stick) butter or margarine, chilled and cut into cubes

SOUR CREAM & ONION CRUNCH

1½ cups sour cream and onion crackers, such as Beigel & Beigel™ Nish Nosh™

¼ cup all-purpose flour

1 Tbsp chopped fresh chives

4 Tbsp (½ stick) butter or margarine, chilled and cut into cubes

SMOOTH & CHUNKY FILLINGS

Fill your challahs with extra yumminess!
Savory or sweet, the following recipes will take your challahs to the next level.
See page 259 for instructions on filling a challah.

FIG FILLING

1½ cups chopped fresh or dried figs

½ cup water

¼ cup orange juice

¼ cup sugar

½ tsp cinnamon

¼ tsp fine sea salt

1. Add all the ingredients to a medium saucepan over high heat.
2. Bring to a boil, then lower heat and simmer until most of the liquid has dissolved and thickened, 10-15 minutes. Stir occasionally to prevent sticking.

3. Allow the mixture to cool slightly. Transfer to a food processor fitted with the S-blade; pulse for a few seconds to make a coarse paste. Store in an airtight container in the fridge for up to 1 month.

SPINACH WALNUT PESTO FILLING

4 cups fresh spinach

¼ cup toasted walnuts

1 small clove garlic, chopped

2 tsp fresh lemon juice

¼ tsp crushed red pepper flakes

3 Tbsp olive oil

1 ounce grated Parmesan cheese, optional

Add all the ingredients to a food processor fitted with the S-blade; pulse until smooth, leaving a bit of a chunky texture. Store in an airtight container in the fridge for up to 1 week.

SWEET POPPY FILLING

1½ cups full-fat coconut milk

1 cup sugar

1 tsp vanilla extract

Zest of 1 lemon

Zest of 1 orange

1 cup poppy seeds

⅔ cup ground almonds

⅔ cup ground walnuts

1. Add the coconut milk, sugar, vanilla, lemon zest, and orange zest to a saucepan over high heat.

2. Bring to a boil, then stir in the poppy seeds. Lower heat and simmer for 5 minutes. Stir occasionally to prevent sticking.

3. Add the ground nuts, and stir to combine. Remove from heat.

4. Allow to cool, then refrigerate. The mixture will thicken up when cold. Store in an airtight container in the fridge for up to 1 month.

CARAMELIZED ONIONS

½ cup oil

4 large yellow onions, diced

1 tsp fine sea salt

1. Heat the oil in a frying pan over medium heat. Add onions, and sauté for 5 minutes or until starting to soften.

2. Add the salt, reduce heat to medium-low, and cook for about 1 hour, stirring every few minutes, until the onions are very soft, golden brown, and caramelized. Store in an airtight container in the fridge for up to 1 week.

GARLIC CONFIT

This is more of a technique than an exact recipe, so adjust the amount of garlic cloves and pan size depending on how much garlic confit you want to make. The pan should be big enough for the garlic to be in a single (yet cozy) layer.

Peeled garlic cloves

Olive Oil

Kosher salt (to taste)

1. Preheat the oven to 375°F. Add garlic cloves to a baking dish.

2. Pour olive oil over the cloves to cover. Season with a pinch of kosher salt.

3. Roast, uncovered, for 30 minutes, until garlic is golden brown and softened. Store in an airtight container in the fridge for up to 2 weeks.

COMPOUND BUTTERS

If you've ever had a slice of hot challah smeared with butter, you already know that there are very few things in the world that can compete. But what if those butters were flavored with herbs, spices, lemon zest, or sweet syrups? Well then, plain ole' butter may have met its match. Compound butter is simply softened butter that is blended with other flavors, and then it is refrigerated to harden again. The result is a spread for challah that wins the gold medal every time!

Herb Butter

Chili Lime Butter

Honey Sriracha Butter

The Method:

1. Bring butter or margarine to room temperature.

2. Add to the bowl of an electric mixer fitted with a whisk attachment; mix until smooth.

3. Add the remaining ingredients to the whipped butter; mix until just incorporated.

4. Transfer butter to a sheet of parchment paper, and roll up to form a log (about 2 inches in diameter). Seal the ends by twisting the paper.

5. Refrigerate for at least 30 minutes to harden.

6. Remove from the fridge right before serving, unwrap the paper, and slice the compound butter into rounds. Alternatively, serve the whole log on the table.

RECIPES ON FOLLOWING PAGE

Smoky Butter

Maple Cinnamon Butter

Lemon Basil Butter

Rosemary Kalamata Butter

COMPOUND BUTTERS

YIELD: 1 ROLL COMPOUND BUTTER

Challah is usually served with a meat meal, so I highly recommend making these butters non-dairy. Instead of butter, I like to use Earth Balance™ or Smart Balance™, which are non-dairy buttery spreads. Any non-dairy butter substitute would work perfectly with all of these recipes.

HERB BUTTER

½ cup (1 stick) unsalted butter, at room temperature

2 Tbsp chopped fresh herbs, such as parsley, thyme, rosemary, and oregano

1 tsp fine sea salt

CHILI LIME BUTTER

½ cup (1 stick) unsalted butter, at room temperature

2 Tbsp lime zest

1 Tbsp finely chopped cilantro, optional

½ tsp chili powder

½ tsp fine sea salt

HONEY SRIRACHA BUTTER

½ cup (1 stick) unsalted butter, at room temperature

1 Tbsp honey

1 Tbsp Sriracha, or to taste

2 cloves garlic, finely minced

½ tsp fine sea salt

MAPLE CINNAMON BUTTER

½ cup (1 stick) unsalted butter, at room temperature

3 Tbsp maple syrup

1 Tbsp confectioners' sugar

1 tsp cinnamon

½ tsp fine sea salt

ROSEMARY KALAMATA BUTTER

½ cup (1 stick) unsalted butter, at room temperature

½ cup pitted kalamata olives, finely chopped

1 Tbsp minced fresh rosemary

LEMON BASIL BUTTER

½ cup (1 stick) unsalted butter, at room temperature

½ cup finely chopped fresh basil

1 clove garlic, finely minced

1 Tbsp lemon zest

½ tsp fine sea salt

¼ tsp freshly ground black pepper

SMOKY BUTTER

½ cup (1 stick) unsalted butter, at room temperature

1 Tbsp minced fresh rosemary

2 tsp smoked paprika

½ tsp fine sea salt

THE DELIGHTFUL WORLD OF CHALLAH

THE SHAPES & COLORS OF CHALLAH

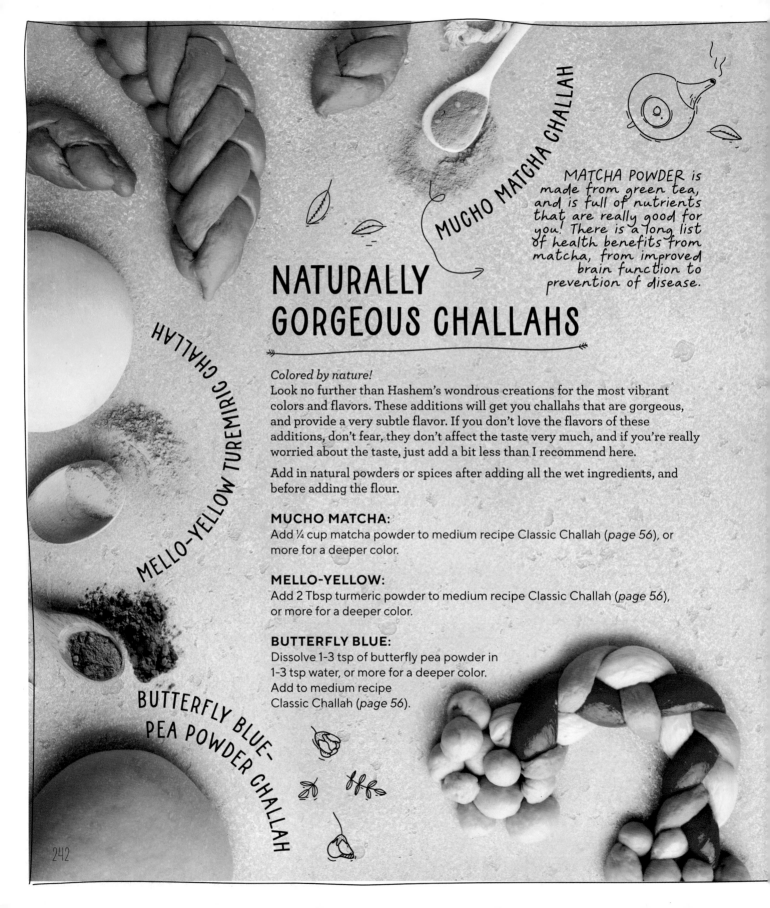

MUCHO MATCHA CHALLAH

MATCHA POWDER is made from green tea, and is full of nutrients that are really good for you! There is a long list of health benefits from matcha, from improved brain function to prevention of disease.

NATURALLY GORGEOUS CHALLAHS

Colored by nature!

Look no further than Hashem's wondrous creations for the most vibrant colors and flavors. These additions will get you challahs that are gorgeous, and provide a very subtle flavor. If you don't love the flavors of these additions, don't fear, they don't affect the taste very much, and if you're really worried about the taste, just add a bit less than I recommend here.

Add in natural powders or spices after adding all the wet ingredients, and before adding the flour.

MUCHO MATCHA:
Add ¼ cup matcha powder to medium recipe Classic Challah (*page 56*), or more for a deeper color.

MELLO-YELLOW:
Add 2 Tbsp turmeric powder to medium recipe Classic Challah (*page 56*), or more for a deeper color.

BUTTERFLY BLUE:
Dissolve 1-3 tsp of butterfly pea powder in 1-3 tsp water, or more for a deeper color. Add to medium recipe Classic Challah (*page 56*).

MELLO-YELLOW TUREMIRIC CHALLAH

BUTTERFLY BLUE– PEA POWDER CHALLAH

ROYALLY RED BEET CHALLAH

One of nature's brightest hues, the deep red of this amazing root vegetable gives us a clue into how healthy it is for us! From deep fuschia to bright red, beets will make your challah gorgeous. Here's how to make a challah that is vibrant and stunning!

BEET CHALLAH RECIPE:

1-1¼ cups beet purée *(recipe follows)*
Medium recipe Classic Challah *(page 56)*, with the following variations:
- Use 1¾ cups water instead of 2 cups
- Add the puréed beets with the wet ingredients, before the flour is added.
- Increase the amount of flour as needed
  (you will likely end up using 8-9 cups of flour).

Prepare the beet purée in advance:
1. Preheat oven 400°F. Wrap beets loosely in foil; roast for 1 hour, until fork tender. Allow to cool.
2. Once cool enough to handle, unwrap foil. Using gloved hands, push the peels off (they should slide off easily).
3. Roughly chop beets, and transfer to a blender with a few teaspoons of water, only using as much as needed to blend into a thick paste. You should end up with about 1-1¼ cups of blended beets.

THERE ARE LOTS OF NATURAL FOOD COLORING OPTIONS AVAILABLE, WITH KOSHER CERTIFICATION, THAT ARE BETTER FOR YOU THAN THE REGULAR FOOD COLORING. SEE WHAT YOU CAN FIND!

PAINTING CHALLAH

Like the Henna Challah on page 134, painting a challah can be a gorgeous way to create your own challah masterpiece.

CHALLAH "PAINT":

Beat 1 egg yolk with colorings of choice:

For black or brown, add espresso powder or dark chocolate powder.

For bright colors, add gel food coloring until desired color is reached.

PAINTING METHOD:

1. Bake the challah per recipe instructions.
2. When the challah is beginning to brown, but not yet completely cooked (about 8-10 minutes left on the timer), remove from the oven. Using a pastry brush, paint as quickly as possible, being careful to keep the challah warm and not to puncture or deflate it.
3. Reduce the oven temperature to 250-275°F, and continue to bake until golden and cooked through.

EDIBLE DECORATIONS

There are so many ways to decorate a challah!
Here are some of my favorite things to do to make a challah extra special.

DECORATIVE DOUGH:

¾ cup flour

¼ cup water

1 Tbsp sugar

1. Mix flour, water, and sugar in a bowl, and knead until a dough is formed.
2. Round out the ball of dough, then wrap in plastic wrap.
   Refrigerate for at least 30 minutes.
3. Using a rolling pin, roll the dough flat.
4. Using a sharp paring knife or little cookie cutters, cut out desired shapes.
5. Glaze with egg, then sprinkle on some coarse sugar (if desired).
6. Place decorations on an unbaked challah, and bake challah as usual.

FREEZE DRIED FRUIT OR BERRIES:

For extra color, flavor, and crunch, top challah with crushed
freeze-dried strawberries or raspberries!

EDIBLE FLOWERS:

Try topping your challah with edible flowers like
rose petals, chamomile, or lavender.

"Dip the apple in the honey, make a bracha loud and clear, L'shana tova u'metukah, have a happy sweet new year!"

This song plays on repeat in my house (and in my head) all through the preparations for Rosh Hashanah, the beginning of the Jewish New Year. Rosh Hashanah means "the head of the year," and just like our heads contain everything that will happen in our bodies, Rosh Hashanah is the time when everything that will happen in the coming year is brought down to us in potential, for us to access and draw from throughout the year to come.

We focus on feeling confident and joyful that we will only receive beautiful sweet blessings in the coming year, and we eat lots of special foods to help us feel the sweetness that is coming our way. We dip our challah and apples (see the song above!) into sweet honey, and say a special blessing that we should be renewed for a good and sweet year.

These little mini apples are just too adorable. Dip them into honey, and you have the perfect combo of all things Rosh Hashanah, sweetness, apples, and challah—all rolled into one!

HOW TO MAKE IT!

1. Grease mini non-stick egg tart molds.
2. Shape dough into balls and place in tart molds.
3. Cut pretzel sticks to size and push into the center for the stem.
4. Allow to rise until very puffy, then glaze with egg and bake. Add a bay leaf for decoration after baking.

ROSH HASHANAH
MINI APPLES

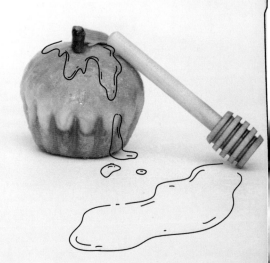

HOW TO MAKE IT!

1. Shape a large Twisted Turban (*page 258*).
2. Make a bird-shaped challah (*page 282*).
3. Place bird on top of spiral, glaze with egg, and bake as usual.

YOM KIPPUR
BIRD ON SPIRAL CHALLAH

Yom Kippur is the holiest day of the year. We don't eat or drink, we wear white like angels, and we try to stay focused and connected to the spiritual world. Before the fast begins, there is a special feast that we make—the final meal before Yom Kippur. At this meal, we eat different symbolic foods to remind us of the importance of the day that is about to begin.

Throughout the ages, Jewish women would shape their challah into a spiral throughout the month of holidays that includes Rosh Hashanah and Yom Kippur to remind us of the cycle of life and the opportunity to return to our roots at any moment. Just like there is no start and end to a circle, we can always enter into a new beginning at any moment in time.

For the meal before Yom Kippur, the Jewish women of old would add a bird on top of the spiral to represent Hashem's protection of us, just like a mother bird protects her baby chicks. Here is a "twist" on the classic spiral challah, with a mama bird perched right on top.

May all of our prayers be answered, and may we feel Hashem's love and protection in our lives at every moment.

HOW TO MAKE IT!

First, color the dough as desired. A great natural coloring option for the green is matcha powder and turmeric for yellow (*page 242*).

THE LULAV:
Roll out a large rectangle of dough with a rolling pin.
Using a pizza cutter, slice into thin strips.
Layer the strips on top of each other.

THE HADASIM & ARAVOT:
Roll two long strands and two medium strands.
Cut Epi-style (*page 105*).

THE RINGS:
Make three long braids to wrap around the lulav.

THE ESROG:
Shape the dough into an esrog-shaped ball.
Place a clove in the narrower top.

After the intensity of the High Holidays, Rosh Hashanah and Yom Kippur, Sukkot is a time to relax and rejoice! We build a temporary hut outside our homes called a *sukkah*, where we eat all our meals, singing and celebrating the new year and all its blessings. We invite everyone to join us in our *sukkah*, and we pray that we will all be reunited soon under one *sukkah* together.

Besides sitting in the *sukkah*, we also do another *mitzvah* for Sukkot, which involves shaking and making a special blessing on the *lulav* and *esrog*. An *esrog* (or *etrog*) is a special citrus fruit, the *lulav* is a palm branch, tall and wavy, which we bind together with willow leaves and myrtle branches to create the complete *lulav* set.

These four species combined—the *esrog*, *lulav*, *hadasim* (myrtle) and *aravot* (willow), represent all types of people. As we hold them all together and say a blessing, we think about uniting all of humanity, creating a world of peace and harmony.

SUKKOT
LULAV AND ESROG CHALLAH

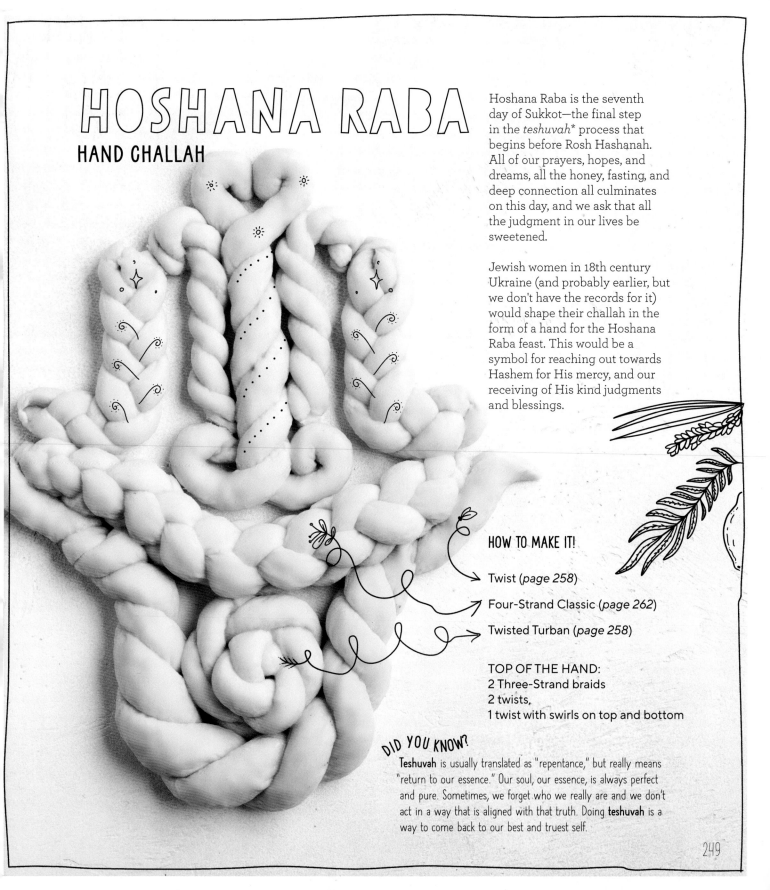

HOSHANA RABA

HAND CHALLAH

Hoshana Raba is the seventh day of Sukkot—the final step in the *teshuvah** process that begins before Rosh Hashanah. All of our prayers, hopes, and dreams, all the honey, fasting, and deep connection all culminates on this day, and we ask that all the judgment in our lives be sweetened.

Jewish women in 18th century Ukraine (and probably earlier, but we don't have the records for it) would shape their challah in the form of a hand for the Hoshana Raba feast. This would be a symbol for reaching out towards Hashem for His mercy, and our receiving of His kind judgments and blessings.

HOW TO MAKE IT!

Twist (*page 258*)

Four-Strand Classic (*page 262*)

Twisted Turban (*page 258*)

TOP OF THE HAND:
2 Three-Strand braids
2 twists,
1 twist with swirls on top and bottom

DID YOU KNOW?

Teshuvah is usually translated as "repentance," but really means "return to our essence." Our soul, our essence, is always perfect and pure. Sometimes, we forget who we really are and we don't act in a way that is aligned with that truth. Doing **teshuvah** is a way to come back to our best and truest self.

Chanukah is the holiday that celebrates the miracle of our spiritual survival. The ancient Greeks tried to persuade the Jewish people to let go of the idea of G-d and spirituality. They wanted the Jews to worship the physical world like they did. But the Jews believed in Hashem and were faithful to His Torah and *Mitzvot*.

So we went to war to fight for our survival. And miraculously, even though we were a tiny army against a huge one, we won. We came back into our holy Temple, which was vandalized and neglected, and we reclaimed it as our own. The first act of rededication was to light the Menorah in the Temple, which was always supposed to be lit. But the pure oil we needed was ruined, only one tiny jar of oil was found, and it would take eight days to get more oil to the Temple.

We lit it anyway—with great faith—and the oil lasted for eight days.

To remember the miracle of our faith and survival, we light the Menorah for eight days every Chanukah. We also eat lots of food fried in oil and play dreidel, the spinning toy that has the secret message on it... "A great miracle happened there." *Oh, and now you can make a challah Menorah—that's like having your miracle and eating it too!*

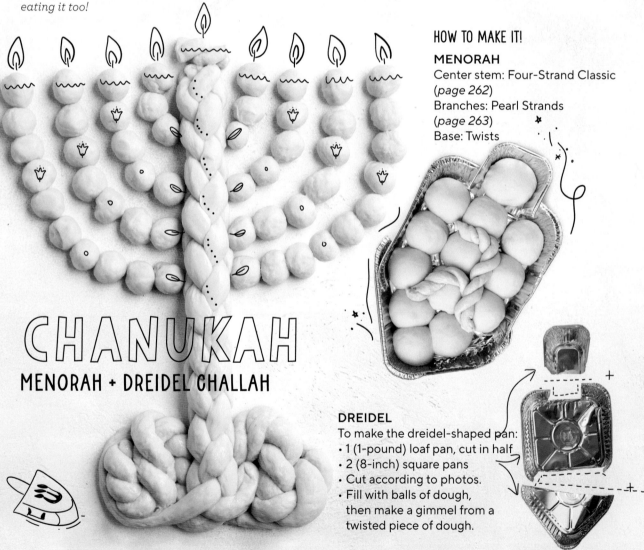

CHANUKAH
MENORAH + DREIDEL CHALLAH

HOW TO MAKE IT!

MENORAH
Center stem: Four-Strand Classic
(*page 262*)
Branches: Pearl Strands
(*page 263*)
Base: Twists

DREIDEL
To make the dreidel-shaped pan:
• 1 (1-pound) loaf pan, cut in half
• 2 (8-inch) square pans
• Cut according to photos.
• Fill with balls of dough, then make a gimmel from a twisted piece of dough.

TU B'SHVAT

FIG FILLED POMEGRANATE CHALLAH

HOW TO MAKE IT!

To color the dough naturally, use the beet coloring method (*page 243*) or use food coloring.

Cut the white part of a leek into 1½ inch rings.

Using scissors, cut the tops of the rings into a crown shape.

Shape the colored dough into round balls.
Using your fingers, open a hole in the center and fill with Fig Filling (*page 234*). Pinch the top shut.

Press the leek crowns into the top of the balls of dough.

Glaze with egg white only (to preserve the color), then bake as usual.

Tu B'shvat is the New Year for the trees. It is a time to celebrate the bounty of fruits and vegetables that Hashem gives us, and we try to eat some of the seven special fruits of the Land of Israel. One of these fruits is the *rimon*, the pomegranate. The Jewish people are compared to the *rimon* because just as it is filled with so many beautiful seeds, every Jewish person is filled with *mitzvot* and goodness, ready to plant light and warmth in another person's heart.

Another fruit of the Land of Israel is the fig, and we incorporated that into this gorgeous challah by filling the middle with a delicious fig spread.

Sometimes Tu B'Shvat lands on a Shabbat. In that case, this challah would be a great way to bring them both together.

While Chanukah celebrates the survival of our spirit, Purim celebrates the very survival of the Jewish people. The tale of Purim sounds like a great play, with lots of drama, tragedy, and victory, but when you read the story in the *Megillah*, the name of Hashem does not even appear once. Purim is all about kings and queens and palace intrigue. One thing just seems to lead to the next, and in the end, you realize that all the pieces fell into place so perfectly that it was clearly the hand of Hashem that was there all along. Our Sages teach us that the *Megillah* is like a detective story, where we have to uncover Hashem's role in the story, but there are clues if you know how to look. Every time it talks about the king in the Megillah, it's actually hinting at the King of all Kings… yup, that's Hashem! And just like we uncover the miracles in the story of Purim, we try to be detectives in our own lives— seeing the miracles that happen to us every single day.

HOW TO MAKE IT!

- Shape a large portion of dough into a ball the size of the crown. Roll it in some water, then dip into poppy seeds until fully coated.

- Shape another portion of dough about ¾ of the size of the first one. Using a rolling pin, roll it out into a large, flat circle. Place the poppy covered dough on top of the flat circle.

- Using a bench scraper or pizza cutter, cut strips about 1" wide around the diameter of the flat circle. Using your hands, create an opening in the top of the large dough ball, kind of like a doughnut.

- Braid sets of three strips together from the dough circle, then wrap them up and over the large dough ball into the hole in the center.

- Place a maraschino cherry in the hole in the center.

- Roll two long strands of dough. Dip one into poppy seeds and one into sesame seeds, then twist together and wrap around the circumference of the crown.

PURIM
CROWN CHALLAH

POST-PESACH

SHLISSEL CHALLAH

In the desert, as the Jewish people journeyed to the Holy Land, they were fed by Hashem the *manna* from heaven. It fell each day for 40 years, except on Shabbat. On Friday, a double portion would fall, giving them enough to last through Shabbat. When they finally arrived in the Land of Israel, they kept the first Pesach in the Holy Land and brought the *omer* offering on the second day of the holiday. This was a grain offering, which signified that they would now begin to farm, plant, and harvest their own food. No longer would the *manna* fall from heaven and sustain them. Pesach became the time to pray for a year in which we receive plenty of grains (food!). We ask that the gates of Heaven be opened for us along with an outpouring of blessings into our lives.

The Talmud also states that Pesach is the "new year" for the judgment of the grains. So the judgment on how much grain we will receive that year happens on Pesach.

Shlissel challah (which means key challah, in Yiddish) is an ancient custom, wherein the Jewish women would braid their challahs into the shape of a key, or place an actual key in their challah (or both!). This is done on the Shabbat that follows Pesach, as we reintroduce bread back into our lives after a week of being *chametz*-free.

These days, it has become very popular to make key challahs, and the variations that have circulated on social media are just astounding! Here are some fun shapes that are meant to inspire you to come up with your very own *shlissel challah* creation.

HOW TO MAKE IT!

These challahs were all made using lines, swirls, twists, or basic three-strand braids.
Get creative and have fun!

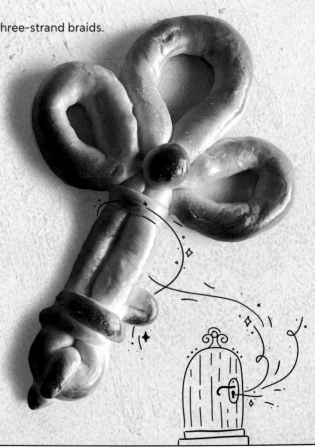

POST-PESACH
SHLISSEL CHALLAH

The Jewish people—women, men, and children—would sing and dance their way up the hills to Jerusalem. They were dressed in their finest, and their horses and donkeys would be draped in flowers. They would carry baskets woven of the shiniest gold on their shoulders, overflowing with the first of their fruits and their most beautiful stalks of wheat. This was their *bikurim* offering for the holiday of Shavuot. Shavuot, which comes at the very beginning of summer, is the celebration of the day we received the Torah on Mount Sinai and also a celebration of the grain harvest. We would reconnect with the Source of our gifts by taking the first fruits that grew (the best of everything we had) and bringing them up to the *Beit Hamikdash*. On Shavuot, the offering was the "*shtei halechem*," two loaves of risen bread, made from the stalks of wheat that were brought up to the Temple, which was one of the only times bread was brought as an offering.

This basket, made of the shiniest golden challah, from the finest wheat, is a beautiful way to remember this celebration of baskets, bread, and bounty! You can fill it with fruits as a Shavuot holiday centerpiece or even with more challah!

HOW TO MAKE IT!

See step-by-step instructions for making this challah basket on page 277.

SHAVUOT
"BIKURIM" BASKET CHALLAH

BRAID THIS BOOK!

THE
SHAPES
OF CHALLAH

BEAUTIFUL BRAIDS START WITH BEAUTIFUL STRANDS!

Here's how to make that happen.

> SOME HELPFUL TOOLS FOR BRAIDING AND SHAPING YOUR CHALLAH!
>
> ♥ Bench scraper
> ♥ Rolling pin
> ♥ Kitchen scale
> ♥ Silicone mat
> ♥ Scissors
> ♥ Pizza cutter

1 Start by dividing your dough into portions. Round off each portion of dough by rolling it in your hand or on a smooth surface, tucking as you roll so that the messy part ends up on the underside of the rolled piece.

2 Cover the dough, and allow it to rest while you work with the remaining portions.

> ## LET YOUR CHALLAH DOUGH REST
>
> After you pull off a piece of dough and round it, it needs some resting time, so the gluten strands can relax again, and it will be easy to roll into any shape.

3 Now we roll the strands — always on a surface, never in the air. For a tapered challah, roll a little harder on the outer ends of the strand to create thinner ends.

4 If you want a really smooth strand, roll a ball of dough into a long rectangle, then roll it up lengthwise.

BASIC SHAPES AND TECHNIQUES

THE BASIC TWIST

THE ONE-STRAND TWIST

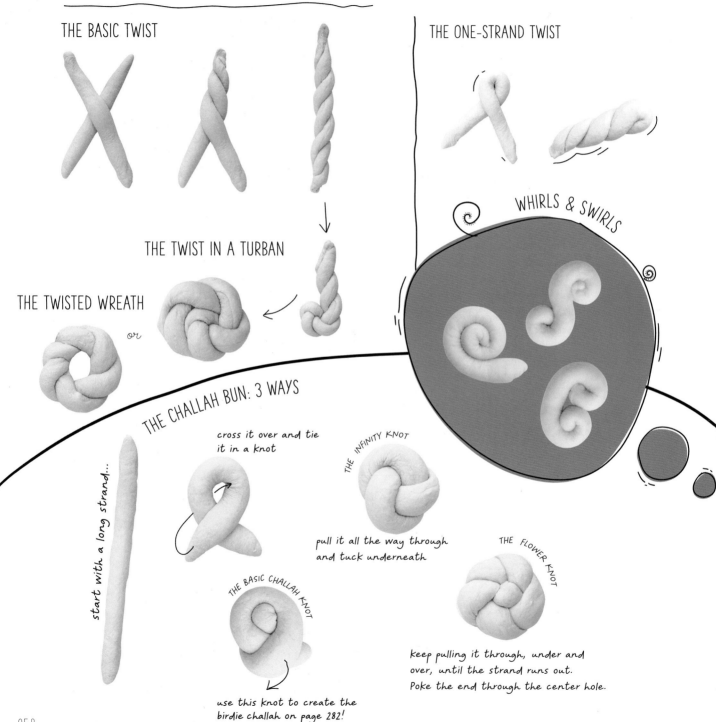

THE TWIST IN A TURBAN

WHIRLS & SWIRLS

THE TWISTED WREATH

or

THE CHALLAH BUN: 3 WAYS

start with a long strand...

cross it over and tie it in a knot

THE INFINITY KNOT

pull it all the way through and tuck underneath

THE FLOWER KNOT

THE BASIC CHALLAH KNOT

keep pulling it through, under and over, until the strand runs out. Poke the end through the center hole.

use this knot to create the birdie challah on page 282!

FILLING A STRAND WITH SOMETHING YUMMY

Filling the strands of dough is a great way to add extra flavor and color to your challah.
Go savory — like the pesto pictured here — or go sweet; either way, you can't go wrong! See page 234 for filling ideas.

DIPPING THE STRANDS

A beautiful way to add color and texture to your challah is to dip the strands in some water, then roll them around in poppy, sesame, or any seed you like.

CAN YOU THINK OF OTHER FUN THINGS TO COAT YOUR STRANDS IN?
THE MULTIGRAIN GOODNESS CHALLAH ON PAGE 60 HAS LOTS!

THE ONE-STRAND WONDER!

When I do challah braiding demonstrations, this one always gets the loudest oohs and aahs. It's a great little magic trick, where one strand turns into a perfectly braided mini challah. Just follow these pictures to create yours.

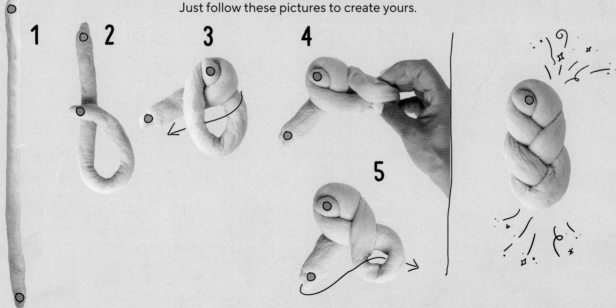

259

TWO STRANDS

FOUR-STRAND BRAID MADE WITH TWO STRANDS!

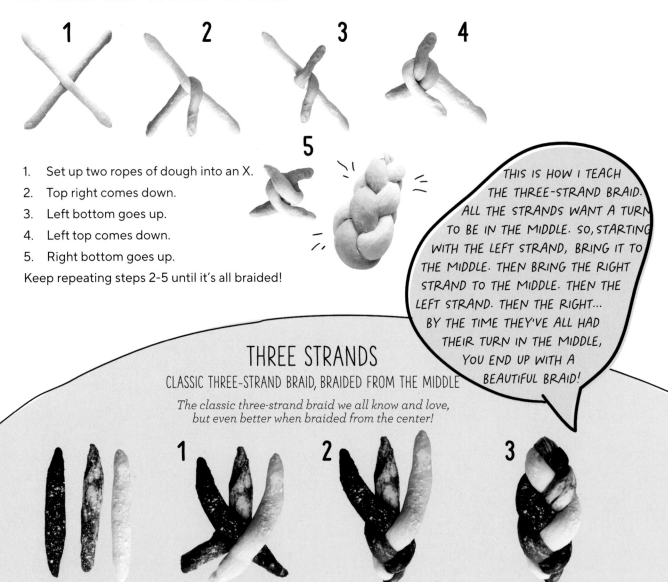

1. Set up two ropes of dough into an X.
2. Top right comes down.
3. Left bottom goes up.
4. Left top comes down.
5. Right bottom goes up.

Keep repeating steps 2-5 until it's all braided!

> THIS IS HOW I TEACH THE THREE-STRAND BRAID. ALL THE STRANDS WANT A TURN TO BE IN THE MIDDLE. SO, STARTING WITH THE LEFT STRAND, BRING IT TO THE MIDDLE. THEN BRING THE RIGHT STRAND TO THE MIDDLE. THEN THE LEFT STRAND. THEN THE RIGHT... BY THE TIME THEY'VE ALL HAD THEIR TURN IN THE MIDDLE, YOU END UP WITH A BEAUTIFUL BRAID!

THREE STRANDS

CLASSIC THREE-STRAND BRAID, BRAIDED FROM THE MIDDLE

*The classic three-strand braid we all know and love,
but even better when braided from the center!*

Braiding from the center of the strands makes a beautiful tapered shape. Start from the center and work down. Then flip the whole thing upside down, with the unfinished strands facing towards you, and braid the second side.

FOUR STRANDS

FOUR-STRAND WEAVE IN A WREATH

1

2

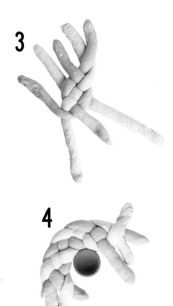

3

4

This is a basic weave braid — over, under, over — except working from one side the whole time.

1. Take the right-most strand and weave through the other three strands — over, under, over.
2. Next, take the new right-most strand and weave in the same pattern — over, under, over.
3. Keep working with the strand that is the farthest to the right, weaving it over, under, over the three strands to the left.
4. Leave the ends loose if you want to turn it into a wreath. Wrap it around an ovenproof bowl, then weave the ends together.

THIS IS MY GO-TO SHAPE WHEN I WANT TO GIFT SOMEONE WITH A CHALLAH. IT MAKES A BEAUTIFUL PRESENTATION. YOU CAN PUT SOMETHING DELICIOUS IN THE MIDDLE TO DIP THE CHALLAH INTO.

FOUR-STRAND CLASSIC

Use the same technique as the classic two-strand on page 260, but here you begin with four strands. The advantage of doing it this way is that the braid ends up tapered on both ends.

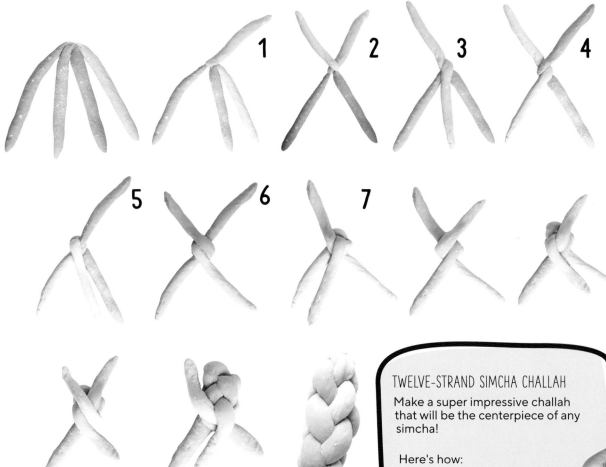

1. Divide the dough into four ropes; connect at the top.
2. Set up the dough into an X as pictured.
3. Bring the top right strand down into the center.
4. Bring the bottom left strand over the top right.
5. Bring the top left strand down into the center.
6. Bring the bottom right strand over the top left.
7. Keep bringing the top strand down and the opposite bottom strand to replace it until your challah is fully formed.

TWELVE-STRAND SIMCHA CHALLAH

Make a super impressive challah that will be the centerpiece of any simcha!

Here's how:
1. Create three of the above four-strand classic braids.
2. Use the same amount of dough for each braid, but roll the strands longer and skinnier for two of them.
3. Put the fatter braid in the center, then lay the two skinnier braids around it. That's it!

FIVE-STRAND FISHTAIL

A fishtail braid is the same as the classic three-strand braid, but here you're working with more strands. This technique works with any uneven number of strands.

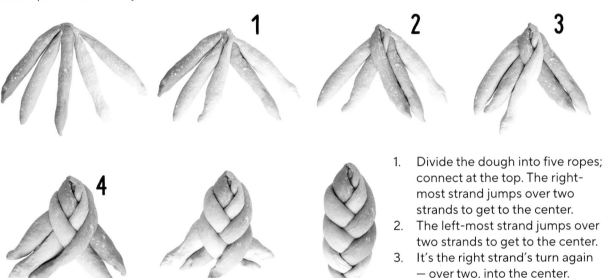

1. Divide the dough into five ropes; connect at the top. The right-most strand jumps over two strands to get to the center.
2. The left-most strand jumps over two strands to get to the center.
3. It's the right strand's turn again — over two, into the center.
4. Now the left takes a turn again — over two, into the center.
5. Repeat until you have a beautiful fishtail braid.

Once you have your beautiful braid, you can have some fun and decorate it! I like to make a little dent in the middle and place a pretty braid or twist on top. Alternatively, try the string of pearls in the center. How pretty is that?

THIS IS A REALLY NEAT TRICK, WHERE ONE LONG STRAND OF DOUGH TURNS INTO A STRING OF PEARLS. I USE THIS FOR THE MENORAH-SHAPED CHALLAH ON PAGE 250 OR TO DECORATE ANY CHALLAH, LIKE THE FIVE-STRAND FISHTAIL HERE.

STRING OF PEARLS

Using the pinky edge of your palm like a knife, make sawing motions back and forth on the strand until a "pearl" is formed — almost until the dough separates, but still has a bit of dough connecting to the rest of the strand. Keep doing this at even intervals until you have a string of challah dough pearls.

FIVE-STRAND TOP TWIST

This is one of the most original braids that lends itself to be manipulated into some beautiful shapes, such as the moon on page 5 and the heart pictured here on the facing page.

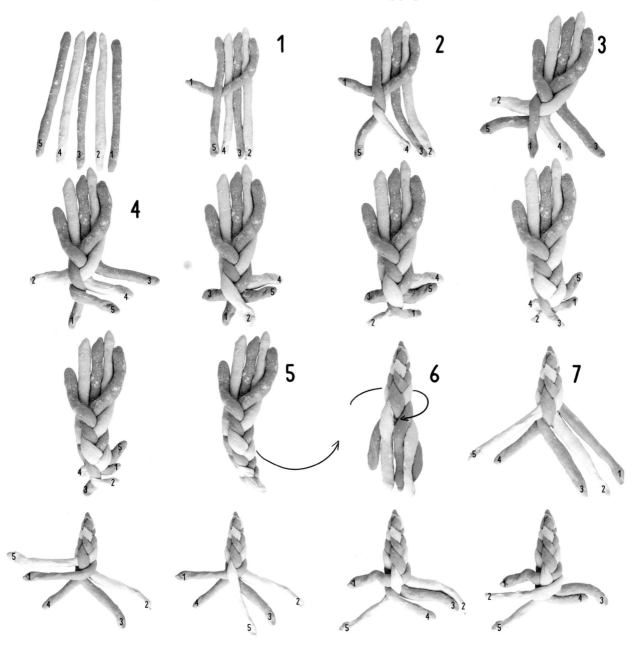

To get the tapered shape, start from the center of the strands. If you want to make it easier when you're first learning this braid, pinch the tops of the strands together and start braiding from the top.

1.   Strand 1 goes over 2, 3, and 4, then under 5.

2.   Strand 4 twists under and around strand 5 to move to the right.

3.   Strand 2 now goes over 3, 4, and 5, then strand 1 comes over it.

4.   Strand 5 twists around strand 1, then moves to the right.

Repeat like this: Outermost right strand crosses over all the strands to the left / The last strand goes over it / The second to last strand twists over to join the right side.

5-6.   If braiding from the center, when one side of the braid is completed, roll it over, then flip over to begin braiding the second end.

7.   Unwind the strands as shown. Renumber the strands to start again from the center down.

Once the braid is complete, roll it over to see how pretty it looks on all sides! Pick the side you like the best. To make the heart, braid a second one the same as the first, then pinch together to create a heart.

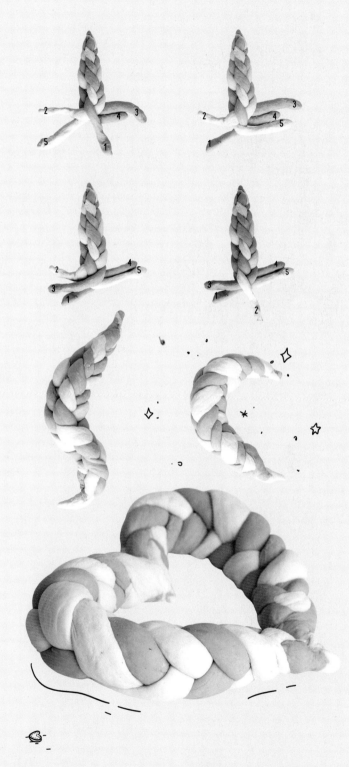

SIX-STRAND CLASSIC

This is THE classic challah shape. When we imagine a challah, this shape is what usually comes to mind! Intricate and beautiful, with height and structure, when you bring this challah out you will always get the oohs and ahhs! This challah uses the same method as the four-strand classic, just with six strands.

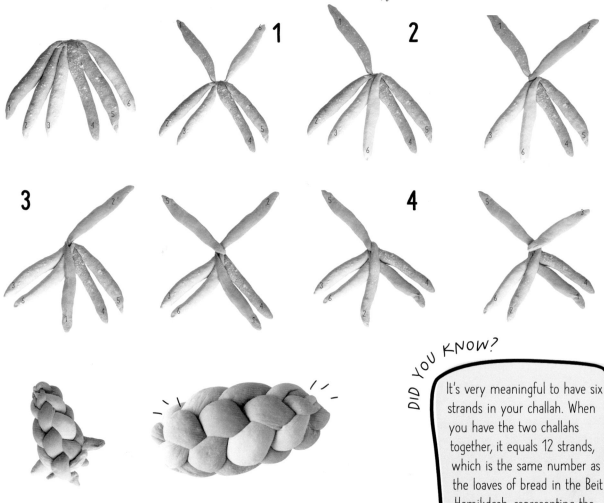

1. Divide the dough into six ropes; connect at the top. Lift strands 1 and 6 to create an X, leaving two strands on each side on the bottom.
2. Starting from the top right, bring strand 6 down into the center, then bring strand 2 up to replace it.
3. Then working from the left side, bring strand 1 down into the center, then bring strand 5 up to replace it.
4. Repeat, bringing the top right strand down into the center, the bottom left strand replacing it, then bringing the top left strand down into the center, the bottom right strand to replace it. Voila! It's a beautiful challah!

DID YOU KNOW?

It's very meaningful to have six strands in your challah. When you have the two challahs together, it equals 12 strands, which is the same number as the loaves of bread in the Beit Hamikdash, representing the 12 tribes of Israel. The love and unity this symbolizes causes the Shechina (Divine presence) to rest on our Shabbat table!

SIX-STRAND WEAVE

This is one of the braids featured in the Bar and Bat Mitzvah Torah challah. The flat shape of the weave lends itself to many different ideas. Can you come up with something interesting? I'd love to see your challah creations. Share them with me online; on facebook or on insta @rochiepinson And maybe I can even repost them for all to be inspired by!

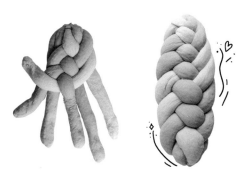

So pretty and so easy!

1. Working from the right side the whole time, go over two strands, under one strand, and over two strands.
2. Repeat until you get a challah that looks like this!

THIS SHAPE IS SO SPECIAL FOR ROSH HASHANAH, WHEN THE TRADITION IS TO MAKE ROUND CHALLAHS. WITH THIS DESIGN YOU CAN HAVE THE ROUND SHAPE WITH THE BEAUTY OF A WEAVE.

SIX-STRAND ROUND BASKET WEAVE

1

2

3

Can you make a three-strand braid? Can you do a basic over/under weave? If so, then you can make this gorgeous basket weave challah.

1-3. Set up your weave as pictured.

4. Braid each section of three strands on each of the four sides.

5. Tuck them under to form a round shape. That's it — you're done.

4

5

6

THE "ROYAL SIX"

This is a gorgeous new braid that I learned from the incredible Idan Chabasov (@challahprince). He is a master of creative braiding, and this is one of his most famous ones. It looks complicated, but just follow the pictures — you can't go wrong.

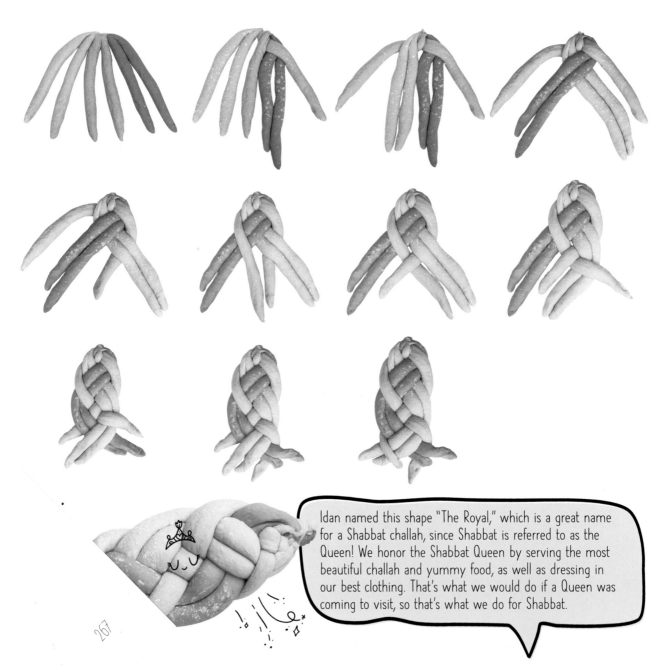

Idan named this shape "The Royal," which is a great name for a Shabbat challah, since Shabbat is referred to as the Queen! We honor the Shabbat Queen by serving the most beautiful challah and yummy food, as well as dressing in our best clothing. That's what we would do if a Queen was coming to visit, so that's what we do for Shabbat.

SEVEN-STRAND WEAVE

Like the six-strand weave, this one is super simple.
1. Starting from the right-most strand, bring it over one strand and under two.
2. Then take the left-most strand, and bring it over one strand and under two. Keep alternating between right and left to create this masterpiece.

NINE-STRAND TRIPLED BASIC

It may be a basic braiding technique, but there's nothing basic looking about this challah!

1. Divide the dough into six thick strands and three narrow strands. Place a narrow strand between two thicker strands. Repeat to make three sets.
2. Proceed to braid like a basic three-strand challah.

For a beautiful presentation, coat the narrow strands (that end up in the middle) with poppy or sesame seeds (see page 259 for technique), or use a different color dough, as pictured here, for the outer, thicker strands.

TWELVE-STRAND ROUND BASKET

This is similar to a four-strand basket weave, but so much fancier. The braiding technique is very simple, even though the result looks complex. This is a beautiful shape for Rosh Hashanah or any time you want something a little different, and very special.

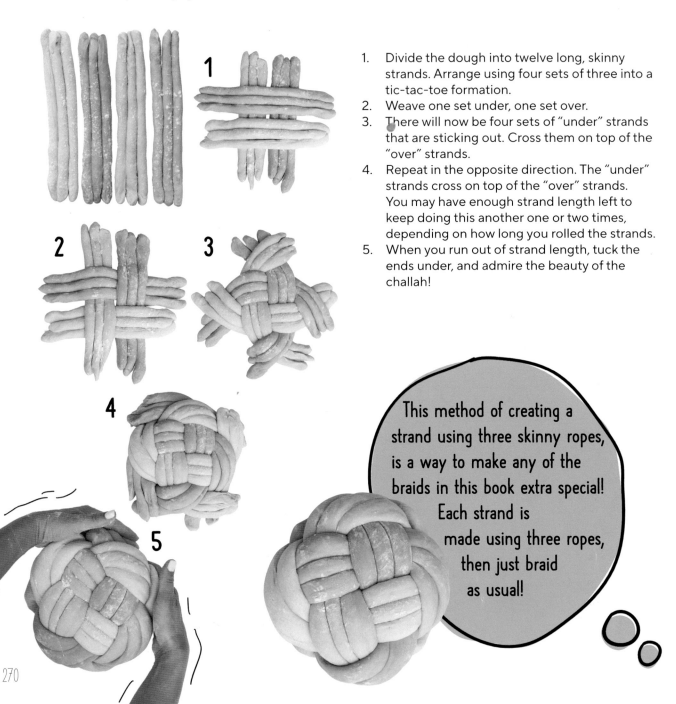

1. Divide the dough into twelve long, skinny strands. Arrange using four sets of three into a tic-tac-toe formation.
2. Weave one set under, one set over.
3. There will now be four sets of "under" strands that are sticking out. Cross them on top of the "over" strands.
4. Repeat in the opposite direction. The "under" strands cross on top of the "over" strands. You may have enough strand length left to keep doing this another one or two times, depending on how long you rolled the strands.
5. When you run out of strand length, tuck the ends under, and admire the beauty of the challah!

This method of creating a strand using three skinny ropes, is a way to make any of the braids in this book extra special! Each strand is made using three ropes, then just braid as usual!

SHAPING A BRIOCHE LOAF

1. Divide the dough into four balls, about 8 ounces each.
2. Using a rolling pin, roll each ball into a rectangle.
3. Roll up each rectangle.
4. Place into a greased loaf pan; bake as directed.

SHAPING A CHALLAH NAPKIN RING

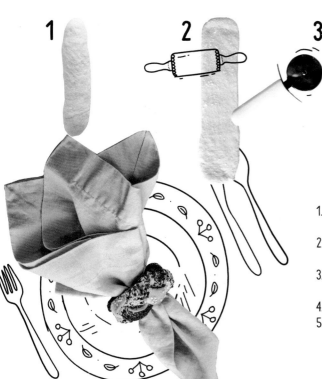

1. Divide the dough into equal portions, depending on the number of challah napkin rings you are making.
2. Using a rolling pin, roll each portion of dough into a long rectangle.
3. Using a pizza cutter, cut each rectangle into three strips.
4. Braid together.
5. Wrap around a well-greased cannoli mold. Place on a baking sheet. Glaze with egg, and top with desired toppings. Bake in a 350°F oven for 15-20 minutes.

SIX STRAND STAR OF DAVID / MAGEN DAVID SHAPE

This braid is just wowza. (My editor says that's not a word. I think it is.) The hole in the center of this shape allows for a dip to be placed in the middle or perhaps honey for Rosh Hashanah.

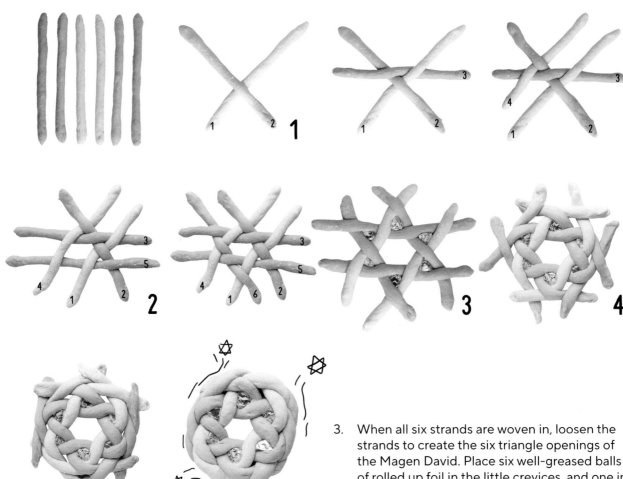

1. Divide the dough into six ropes. Cross two strands over each other to form an X. Follow the pictures weave the remaining strands in, under and over.
2. When you place strand 5, it will be over strand 2, and under strands 1 and 4 — that's the only strand that won't be woven all the way, but it will allow strand 6 to be woven properly.
3. When all six strands are woven in, loosen the strands to create the six triangle openings of the Magen David. Place six well-greased balls of rolled up foil in the little crevices, and one in the center (or a ramekin), to keep them open while baking.
4. Now do an under-over crossover with the long ends of the strands. Working counter clockwise to cross each set of strands, place each "under" strand on top of an "over" strand to its right. Repeat the same thing clockwise.
5. Tuck all the loose ends under. Wowza! This challah is going to be a big hit!

WOVEN HEART CHALLAH

This weave makes the most perfect heart-shaped challah! What a fun idea for an anniversary, wedding, sheva brachot, or just a sweet way to say "I love you" to someone this Shabbat.

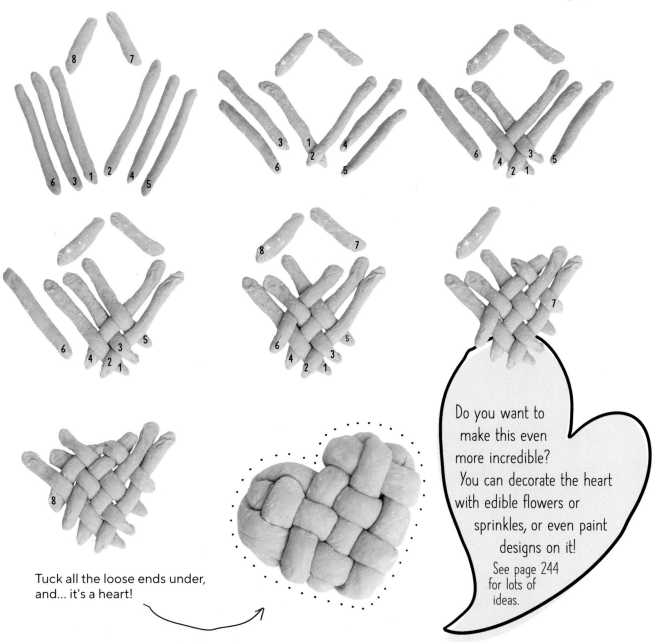

Tuck all the loose ends under, and... it's a heart!

Do you want to make this even more incredible? You can decorate the heart with edible flowers or sprinkles, or even paint designs on it! See page 244 for lots of ideas.

PUMPKIN CHALLAH

Use the Pumpkin Challah recipe on page 74, or transform any challah dough into a magical pumpkin! If making individual-sized pumpkin-shaped challahs, you can use a pecan or cinnamon stick for the stem. If making a full-sized pumpkin-shaped challah, I recommend cutting off the stem from a real pumpkin to decorate your pumpkin challah — a real showstopper!

1. Roll the dough into a smooth ball.

2. Place the ball of dough on top of a large piece of kitchen twine.

3. Bring the twine up and over (as if you're wrapping a ribbon around a gift). Keep the twine a bit loose on the dough, as it will rise and become taut eventually.

4. Keep bringing the twine under the ball and back up, mimicking the sections of a real pumpkin.

5. Allow to rise until puffy.

6. Top with the pumpkin stem (or pecan/cinnamon stick). Bake as directed, then remove the twine while the challah is still warm from the oven.

CHALLAH ROSETTE

Challah rosettes are so pretty. Bake these in muffin cups and serve as individual challah rolls. Alternatively, arrange in a wreath shape, and bake in a round pan.

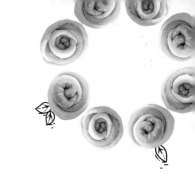

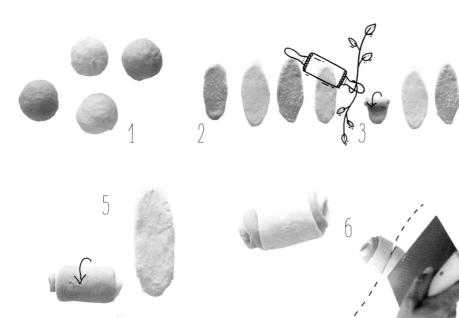

1
2
3
4
5
6
7

1. Round off four small balls of dough for each rosette.

2. Using a rolling pin, roll each ball into an oval shape. Filling these rosettes will make them extra special; if you want to fill them with something, now's the time. Spread the filling over each oval of dough (see filling option in note).

3. Roll up one oval.

4. Place the rolled-up piece on top of a rolled out oval; roll up.

5. Repeat with the remaining two ovals, stacking and rolling. Once you've rolled up all four ovals, you will be left with one log.

6. Using a sharp knife or bench scraper, cut it in half down the middle.

7. Stand them up on the cut end — you'll have two challah rosettes. Repeat the process to make as many challah rosettes as desired.

FILL YOUR CHALLAH ROSETTE WITH APPLE!

✦✦ Using a mandoline or sharp knife, slice unpeeled apples into paper-thin rounds. Lay sliced apples along the length of the ovals, so that the edges of the apple circles come off the sides of the dough. Brush with cinnamon sugar, as well as oil or melted butter. Roll up as instructed above. ✦✦
For more filling ideas,
turn to page 234.

CHALLAH FILLED ROSE

This is a challah flower that you can fill with whatever you'd like. Here I've placed a ball of dough in the center, but I love putting a scoop of something delicious in the center, like pesto for a savory option, or fig filling for sweet (see page 234 for recipes), and creating the rose around it.

1. Using a rolling pin, roll out two balls of dough, then roll each of them into a large circle, rolling one out slightly smaller than the other. Cut four slits into each circle, and place the smaller one on top of the larger one. Top with a small ball of dough.
2. Alternating between the top and bottom layers, lift the pieces of dough and wrap around the center ball. Work from opposite sides each time.
3. Leave two of the pieces unwrapped, then slit through the center of them. Pinch together to create leaves.

PULL-APART CHALLAH FLOWER

Use a springform pan to get the nicest effect, but any round pan will do. Just be sure to grease or line it with parchment paper.

Leave some space between the balls of dough; when they rise, they will come together to create a flower.

BIKURIM CHALLAH BASKET

This stunning basket made of challah dough doesn't require any fancy braiding techniques, but it is tricky to get it right. The payoff however, is well worth it. Have fun!

1.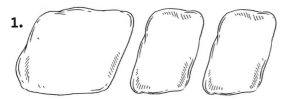

Use approximately 3-5 pounds of dough. It will depend on the size of the bowl you use. Divide the dough into 3 pieces.

2.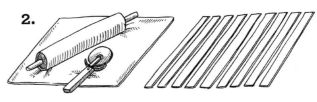

One piece should be double the size of the other 2 pieces. Roll out the largest piece and cut it into long strips.

3.

Lightly grease the outside of an oven-safe bowl. Drape about half of the strips of dough from the center. Use something heavy on top to hold the strands in place; flatten and seal them.

4.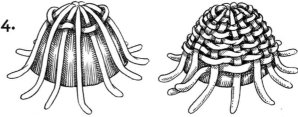

Now, weave the other strips horizontally across the bowl. Don't allow it to rise again once finished. Bake immediately.

5.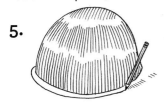

Draw a circle around the bowl you used to bake the basket. Using one of the 2 smaller pieces of dough, make a long three-strand braid and lay it on the circle you drew to ensure it's the right size.

6.

Bake it. Once cooled, attach it to the rim of the basket with toothpicks.

To make the handle, use the third piece of dough, and make another three-strand long, skinny braid. Drape it over the bowl and bake. When cooled, attach it to the basket with toothpicks.

COMING SOON!

TORAH ADVENTURES THRU CHALLAH

EAT THE PARSHA

As a supplement to
The Kids Book of Challah,
Eat The Parsha will have special challah
shapes that represent the stories of
the Torah portions, along with a little
teaching to accompany it.

In the following pages,
I've presented a few of the
shapes that are featured on the
cover of this book, which will be
in the upcoming supplement
accompanied by a parsha teaching.
Look for it in bookstores soon!

THE SHEEP CHALLAH

THE TAIL

2 LEGS

THE FACE

THE BODY

THE HAIR

Many of the great leaders in the Torah started off as shepherds! Moshe (Moses) was a shepherd and saw the burning bush when he was chasing after a wayward sheep. Hashem saw how he had compassion for the little lost sheep, and knew that he would be the caring leader that the Jewish people needed to take them out of slavery.

THE JEWISH PEOPLE ARE OFTEN COMPARED TO SHEEP, AND HASHEM AS OUR SHEPHERD, PROTECTING US FROM ALL THE BIG, BAD WOLVES!

Sprinkle the Lemon Shortbread Streusel or Basic Crumb Streusel (*page 230*) on the body of the sheep to make him nice and "woolly!"

LEOPARD SPOTS CHALLAH

SLICE AND BE AMAZED!

"Yehuda ben Taima said, be **BOLD AS A LEOPARD**, light as an eagle, swift as a deer, and strong as a lion to do the will of your Father in heaven."

The entire code of Jewish Law opens with this statement!
Be bold as a leopard, means to live proudly, and not be intimidated or ashamed by other people's opinions. Just as a leopard doesn't change his spots, we don't change what makes us special and unique just to suit another person's or culture's expectations of us. We stay true to ourselves no matter what! When we stand proudly, keeping the Torah and the mitzvot, then we transform the chutzpah of the leopard into a holy chutzpah, which helps us stand tall and confident and do the will of Hashem with joy and pride.

HOW TO MAKE IT:

1. Divide the dough into 24 balls:
   - 8 (1-ounce) balls of dark black dough (The Cuckoo for Cocoa Challah on page 96 with extra dark cocoa powder will yield a very dark-colored dough.)
   - 8 (1½-ounce) balls of regular Cocoa Challah dough (*page 56*) or whole wheat challah dough (*page 58*).
   - 8 (2½-ounce) balls of regular challah dough.

2. Roll the darkest balls of dough into little logs. Using a rolling pin, roll the white and light brown balls of dough into flat ovals.

3. Wrap a light brown oval of dough over a dark brown log.

4. Wrap a white oval of dough around that. Repeat with the remaining dough.

5. Arrange the logs into a 5-pound loaf pan. Allow to rise until very puffy. Bake in a 350°F oven for 30 minutes. Slice, and be amazed!

PARSHAT VA'ERA

IN THIS WEEK'S PARSHA, THE PLAGUE OF WILD BEASTS COMES UPON EGYPT, TO TEACH PHAROH AND ALL THE PEOPLE, THAT THERE IS ONLY ONE G-D IN THIS WORLD, AND ALL OF CREATION LISTENS TO HIM ALONE. THE WILD BEASTS THAT OVERTAKE EGYPT ARE TERRITORIAL BEASTS LIKE THE LEOPARD, WHO WOULDN'T USUALLY MIX WITH OTHER WILD ANIMALS, BUT BECAUSE THEY ARE SENT BY HASHEM, THEY DEFY THEIR USUAL NATURE TO DO HASHEM'S WILL. SO, IN THIS PARSHA, A LEOPARD REALLY DID CHANGE ITS SPOTS!

CAMEL CHALLAH

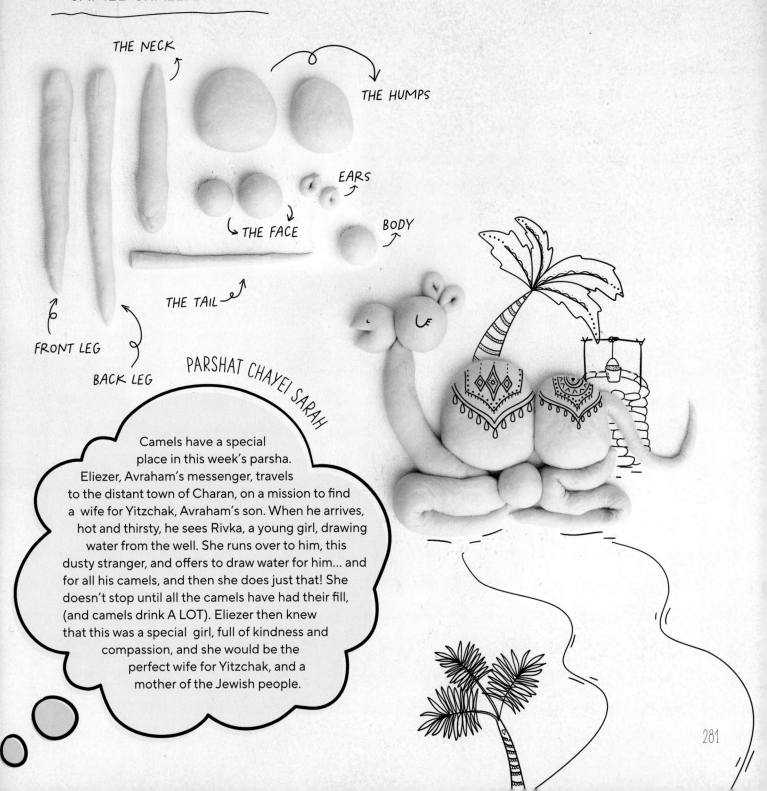

THE NECK

THE HUMPS

EARS

THE FACE

BODY

THE TAIL

FRONT LEG

BACK LEG

PARSHAT CHAYEI SARAH

Camels have a special place in this week's parsha. Eliezer, Avraham's messenger, travels to the distant town of Charan, on a mission to find a wife for Yitzchak, Avraham's son. When he arrives, hot and thirsty, he sees Rivka, a young girl, drawing water from the well. She runs over to him, this dusty stranger, and offers to draw water for him... and for all his camels, and then she does just that! She doesn't stop until all the camels have had their fill, (and camels drink A LOT). Eliezer then knew that this was a special girl, full of kindness and compassion, and she would be the perfect wife for Yitzchak, and a mother of the Jewish people.

BIRD CHALLAH

PARSHAT B'SHALACH

How to make it:

1

2

3

1. Pull the knot out a bit more to make the head of the bird.

2. Flatten the "tail" and make little cuts in it.

3. Add a slivered almond, for a beak, and mini chocolate chips for eyes.

In this week's Parsha, the Jewish people cross the Yam Suf, the "Red Sea" and are saved from the Egyptian army who was coming after them! When they reach the shores on the other side, they burst into song of praise for Hashem for saving them. That's why this Shabbat is called Shabbat Shira, the Shabbat of Song!

There is a tradition to gather the children and tell them the story of this wondrous miracle we experienced, to describe for them the magical way the sea split, bringing forth delicious fruit trees which the children picked from as they sang and danced across the sea, all the while the birds sang along with them these songs of praise. And then the children are given 'kasha' or buckwheat, which they can take outside to feed to the birds, to remind them of the preciousness of all of Hashem's creations, and to honor the birds who sang with us that day, and continue to be the maestros of singing Hashem's praise.

THE KIDS OF THIS BOOK!

I didn't have to go far to find the best models for this book!

My very own nieces and nephews (and kids/grandkids of friends Aden, Faigy, Elisheva, Esther and Yochevad—who are like family) showed up and did the greatest job anyone could do! We had so much fun while they mixed and kneaded and braided and made messes, and I got amazing photos that will help all of you to make the recipes in this book. Thank you to all my sisters, and sisters-in-law, and friends who showed up with their kids (in the required dress code!) and allowed them to be a part of this project. Can you spot the kids here throughout the book?

Rocha · Yetta · Rochel · Rocha · Luba

Esti · Chana · Effi · Ruvi · Yosef

Chaya · Mendel · YakovMo · Rocha · Ella

Temi · Sarah · Sara · Shua · Shneur Z.

Esti · Malka · Rosie · Noah · Bina G.

ACKNOWLEDGMENTS

What a journey this has been!

I want to take a moment to thank my fellow travelers as this cookbook made its way from dream to destination.

With my first cookbook, I was a newbie to the scene, just feeling my way in the dark. It was so gratifying this second time around to be able to have the support of so many in the cookbook and food community. It is truly a special world of caring, connected, and encouraging individuals who I am honored to call friends. Thank you for your help with this book, **Rivky Kleiman** @rivkykleiman_ simplygourmet, **Cheryl Holbert** @nomadbakery, **Vanessa Harper** @lechlechallah, **Idan Chabasov** @challahprince, **Eni** @eniskitchen, **Susie Fishman** @meetmykneads, **Elisheva Taitz** @thatswhatshemade, **Adina Schlass** @the_chefs_wife, and **Shifra** and Shloime Klein @ fleishigsmag. All the cookbook authors, whose acquaintances I have made throughout these past seven years of cookbook writing and food stuff, have shown me such welcome and support. I am grateful to have met you and to have you in my new circle; you are all great inspirations to me.

To my niece **Leah Wineberg (Bryski)**, superstar assistant: Seems like forever ago … you were there at this book's inception. Your assistance in the recipe-testing stage was invaluable. Also—best kids' counselor, coordinator, assistant, and on-set hydrator for the kids' photoshoot: thank you for all the hard work! I hope you feel proud when you see this book.

To my friends and community in Montebello: **Aden Robin**, who had the perfect prop just when I needed it, and saved my photoshoot pre-baking session with a gigantic freezer that will forever be remembered as the best gift I have ever received. **Esther Lapa**, neighbor and friend, **Faigy Gross**, who was there for me in so many ways over this past year, including loaning her gorgeous children, providing perfect props, and even bringing

over food when she knew I wasn't feeding myself! And **Chavi Werzberger**, for coming in at the 11th hour and saving the book. I will forever be grateful to you. And to all of you, my friends and community, for your enthusiasm and support, props, friendship and more.

To **Rebbetzin Rivky Slonim**: Many thanks for the gift of your precious time and sorely needed advice. I trust your wisdom implicitly. *Thank you.*

To all my amazing recipe testers: You answered the call to my recipe-testing requests, and took the time to get it all done—to perfection. I am overwhelmed by your generosity of spirit. **Chloe (Rivkah) Rosen, Salwah Carelse, Shelley Isaacson, Naomi Weinstein, Malky Klein, Susie Fishman, Naama Malomet, Jo Sapir, Rachel Galler, Goldie Barnett, Michal Zisquit, Rena Ne'eman, Deborah Dickson, Marla Klug, Jan Shapiro. Toby Brikman**, you also tested for me, but more than that, you are a true friend. Thank you for your patience with me while I made this book happen— we'll pick up where we left off.

If you tested recipes for me and I missed your name in this list, please forgive me! It is another sleepless night of trying to finish this book. I really am so appreciative of you all.

To my photoshoot team: **Monica Pinto**, you shot my first cookbook and I wouldn't trust anyone else with my dream. You were well-worth the wait, through all the Covid lockdowns and uncertainty. The magnificent photos in this book attest to that. Traveling during scary times and being away from your family for weeks wasn't easy. I'm so grateful for your dedication, through illness and homesickness, and I treasure the time we had together. There is a Higher Power that brought us together, for reasons we are still discovering.

Roizy Elias, photoshoot assistant par excellence. You showed up and gave it your all. It was a pleasure to work with you. I can't wait to .see the great things you'll do. Yocheved Miller, Chana Lerner, Basia and Rochel Leah Schildt, thank you for being part of the dream team! **Chana**, thank you for those coffee runs—they were true lifesavers!

To my other photoshoot team: **Schneur Menaker**, you came in and gave 110%. You brought the book to life with your beautifully lit photography. Your patience and warmth while working with the kids for days on end is the stuff of legends. **Antonia** (and **Artem!**), *who even gets to have friends like these?* I'm so glad your cute *punim* made it into the book, because I always want to remember how incredible you are, to come and devote your teeny tiny bit of energy to kneading all that challah dough (oy!). You're forever immortalized on these pages. **Dasi Gobioff**, you're getting another thank you on the coming page, but I just can't leave you out of this group. You are a special lady, and I feel lucky to know you and blessed to have benefitted from your very special brand of kindness and can-do attitude. Thank you.

To my editors, **Elisheva Taitz** and **Elky Raitport**: You are both astonishing women, accomplishing what most people do as a full-time job somewhere between the hours of no sleep and coffee. Thank you both for caring so much and putting your hearts and souls into this.

To my team at Feldheim, **Eli Meir Hollander** and **Suzanne Brandt**: Thank you for believing in me. *I told you people would buy a challah cookbook!* Now that we're in our third printing and on to a second book, I'm glad your faith in me has paid off.

My family is an endless source of love and encouragement. Thank you Ema and Aba. Thank you Shver and Chaya Leah. Thank you all for being so enthusiastic about this project—and understanding when I went MIA for months to finish this up. I can't wait for this book to live in your homes.

My sisters and sisters-in-law, you are all, as always, my favorite bunch of ladies in the world—for fun, for venting, for sharing all the ups and downs of this and every journey, for props, and, not least, for your gorgeous kids who made the absolute best models (see previous page to meet them all). Special shout out to Shainy for the last-minute testing (and re-testing!)—thank you! To my nieces, sisters, and sisters-in-law who shlepped upstate and dedicated your time during the shoot, thank you!

My kids, ironically all mostly grown up by the time I decided to write a kids' book, are still the best part of my life! **Estee**, thank you for being there in the crunch, shlepping up for the shoot, with nieces in tow, on your one day off, and for always telling it like it is (as a fellow designer!) from a place of love. **Mendel K.**, you joined our family at about the same time as the idea for this book was born—and your enthusiasm for it has been constant. You make our family way better for being a part of it, and we're so grateful for you.

OG **Mendel**, having you around, involved and super enthusiastic for the crazy-town wrap-up of this book is something I will always treasure. Making sure I stayed hydrated, and catching every detail I missed—*how would I have done this without you?* Now at least someone knows the book as well as I do!

Shua, you get your very own sentence in this book. Maybe even a whole paragraph! IN A BOLD FONT. Nobody read (*more like delved into*) my first book more thoroughly than you. It's so much fun to still walk into the kitchen sometimes and see you reading through it—with, of course, all your comments and observations (*especially the skeptical ones! I promise I did make you French toast when you were little, you just don't remember!*). I can't wait to watch you flip through this one and hear your comments. I know they will make me laugh, as you always do!

Avraham, you grew so much as you watched this project grow. It's always fun to see your excitement for the crazy recipes in this book! Also, I'm grateful for all the times you held the camera at weird angles for me, when I know you wanted to be doing anything else! You know there's always some challah in it for you!

I love you all, more than all the challah dough on Earth.

I couldn't have done any of this, or anything for that matter, without my husband's deep support and belief in me. He knew very well what he was in for this time, and he pushed me to do it anyway. That was as brave as it was selfless, and I'm forever grateful.

Finally, and foremost, my gratitude to *Hakadosh Baruch Hu* for His great, unfathomable kindnesses in my life. *Hodu lahashem ki tov.*

THANK YOU!

Chaya Ettlinger and **Miram Schechter**: talented challah bakers & braiders, who volunteered their time to come and patchke with dough in my kitchen. Thank you!

Dasi Gobioff: I don't know what mazel I have that Hashem brought you to me. Meeting you was a highlight of this book, and I have no words to thank you for your extreme dedication, enthusiasm, amazing cooking and baking skills, and simply coming through for me to the next level. Our friendship is an unexpected gift of this book. So grateful for you, and looking forward to getting together without a cookbook involved! May you be blessed.

Eve Singer @broyt_: Like an angel, you shipped out boxes of your most gorgeous props. Asking for nothing, you generously gave of your beautiful items just to enhance this book. Thank you.

Micaela Ezra @ahyin_judaica: You bring only beauty and love to the world with your creativity and your spirit. Thank you for generously loaning your beautiful challah covers. (one of which is peeking into these very words!) Looking forward to more collaboration in the future.

Devorah Leah Jacobson @balloonvangogh:
I asked for a bouquet, and you gave me a garden! You & your balloon art are an inspiration. Thank you!

Faigy Gross: A true friend (and rebbetzin ;). I am so grateful to Hashem that He orchestrated my life so that our paths would intersect. From props to models, to birthday gifts & lunch, for your listening ear, and being my movement motivator. For all this and more, so grateful to have you as a friend and looking forward to the next chapters in the story!

Esty Raskin: Sister by birth, friend by choice! You have been invaluable throughout this journey, your eye for design, and your taste, is impeccable. I'm so grateful for all the valuable direction and time you put into this book, even when you had none to spare. From showing up to the photo shoot and taking over my instagram, (even creating a reel!) to your super encouraging exclamations of joy over the prettiness (Even when we both knew it could still be way better ;)!) Thank you for what you gave to me and to this book. I am lucky and proud to be your sister, you are an inspiration.

Chavi Werzberger: Camera in hand, you came with your fun spirit and amazing smile at the 11th hour, and generously gave of your time and talent, to get this book completed. It was hot, it got late, you had other things to do... but you made it work, because that's who you are. So, so grateful for your contribution to this book. I will never forget your kindness.

ABOUT THE AUTHOR

Rochie Pinson is a rebbetzin of multiple communities, and a teacher and mentor to women locally and around the world. Together with her husband, she co-founded the IYYUN Chabad Center in downtown Brooklyn, New York.

She is a mother, an artist, avid challah baker, and the bestselling author of *Rising! The Book of Challah* (Feldheim, 2017) This is her second book.

Rochie brings a unique blend of wisdom, spiritual awareness, and down-to-earth practicality to the mitzvah of challah. Her voice is humorous, and her energy infectious, as she lectures and leads challah workshops and seminars across the globe.

You can follow her—and her challah journey—through her website at www.therisinglife.net and on facebook and instagram @rochiepinson